THE ALMOST CHURCH

D0369265

OTHER BOOKS BY MICHAEL DURALL

Creating Congregations of Generous People

Beyond the Collection Plate

The Almost Church

Redefining Unitarian Universalism for a New Era

Michael Durall

Foreword by
REV. MARLIN LAVANHAR

JENKIN LLOYD JONES PRESS
AT ALL SOULS UNITARIAN CHURCH
Tulsa, Oklahoma

MICHAEL DURALL
The Almost Church: Redefining Unitarian Universalism For a New Era
www.vitalcongregations.com

Published by Jenkin Lloyd Jones Press at All Souls Unitarian Church,
Tulsa, Oklahoma

Copyright ©2004 by Jenkin Lloyd Jones Press at All Souls Unitarian Church

All rights reserved.

Editing: Jean Caffey Lyles
Design and production: Polly Christensen
Cover Design: Bonnie Mettler

No part of this work may be reproduced or transmitted in any form or by any
means, electronic or mechanical, including photocopying and recording, or by any
information storage or retrieval system, except as may be permitted by the 1976
Copyright Act or in writing from the publisher. Requests for permission should be
addressed to:

> Jenkin Lloyd Jones Press
> at All Souls Unitarian Church
> 2952 South Peoria Avenue
> Tulsa, OK 74114

ISBN-0-9755389-0-X

CONTENTS

To those who seek a strengthened faith

FOREWORD

THE PUBLISHING OF THIS BOOK fulfills two dreams. The first is to establish Jenkin Lloyd Jones Press to publish the most innovative voices in Unitarian Universalism today, and in the years to come. There is a recognizable need for a mission-based Unitarian Universalist press that will ensure critical writings are made available on topics of utmost concern to the future of liberal religion.

The second dream is to publish this particular book, a prophetic call to visionary souls within Unitarian Universalism. The beginning of the twenty-first century has the potential to be the most enlivening period in the history of Unitarian Universalism. It also has the potential to be the most disappointing. At a time when many of the core values and messages of Unitarian Universalism are embraced by an increasing number of religious groups and by society at large, most UU churches are on plateaus or in decline in membership.

Unitarian Universalism is an innovative and creative faith tradition, yet we risk becoming out of touch with the spiritual and religious needs of our members and our communities. This book offers thoughtful insights that clergy and lay leaders within Unitarian Universalism need to read, ponder, and act upon.

In this, his third book, Michael Durall utilizes his extensive experience as a church consultant who works with numerous denominations. He gleans the writings of forward-looking thinkers in religious life in America today, and applies what he has learned to Unitarian Universalism. Durall encourages us to "write a new playbook" by which we can create the UU church of tomorrow.

I have no doubt this book will prod, upend, upset, inspire and instigate new ideas among those who care about the future of Unitarian Universalism. In it you will find a vision for multicultural congregations that defy conventional UU wisdom. You will also be

persuaded to urge your congregation to offer its members a powerful vision of the good life—a compelling alternative to a life of af-
fluence. Imagine creating high expectation UU churches that stir
their members to take risks, confront who they truly are, and
become the kind people the church calls them to become.

Durall has taken the sugarcoating off the accustomed self-
assessments that UUs are used to hearing, and in this book he does
it extremely well.

—REVEREND MARLIN LAVANHAR,
Senior Minister, All Souls Unitarian Church,
Tulsa, Oklahoma.

Acknowledgements

I AM VERY APPRECIATIVE of The Reverend Marlin Lavanhar and All Souls Unitarian Church in Tulsa, Oklahoma, for founding the Jenkin Lloyd Jones Press, and for publishing this book.

I am particularly grateful to the many clergy, lay leaders, and people in the pews who shared their hopes, dreams, and yearnings for a more engaging faith.

*"Today's church
is incapable of responding
to the present moral crisis.
It must reinvent itself
or face virtual oblivion
by mid-twenty-first century."*

—GEORGE BARNA,
from his book
The Second Coming of the Church

Introduction

NITARIAN UNIVERSALISM is a movement that is desperately in need of a greater purpose. Despite its strengths, our faith tradition has been compromised by the attempt to be all things to all people, and to offend no one. In doing so, we have lost sight of the meaning of religion today. This book is intended to help reclaim the importance and the value of the Unitarian Universalist faith.

Let's begin with local congregations. To be sure, UU churches are places where people can find their spirits renewed. However, many congregations live in the past. In most churches the traditional order of service has remained unchanged for decades. Many of the hymns we sing date from the 1800s. In reading newsletters from churches across the country I find similar subjects repeated in sermon topics and church programs year after year. The UU church of today looks and feels remarkably similar to the one I joined in 1976.

In addition, few UU churches have more than a token line item in the budget for outreach, which means they spend most of the money they raise on themselves. Money raised is for institutional maintenance and little more. The result is that many UU churches are places of self-enlightenment and entertainment for middle class people who are already there.

Unitarian Universalism is not the only faith tradition in this quandary. George Barna, a prominent author and keen observer of religious life, notes a parallel trend in mainline Protestantism. He writes, "When all factors are objectively assessed, the picture looks pretty much the same as usual; mostly small congregations involved in an unchanging set of programs and events designed to satisfy a well-defined, consistent group of needs relative to a rather circumscribed set of people." [1]

A friend of mine is a minister of the United Church of Christ, and she underscored Barna's view when she said, "My son, now in his twenties, wouldn't set foot in the church I serve. He thinks it's the church of yesterday, for his parents and grandparents."

Anyone who has attended a highly interactive youth worship service at a Unitarian Universalist General Assembly or a youth "Con" (conference) has probably come to the realization that younger generations are unlikely to seek a church in which traditional worship, nineteenth-century music, and fixed pews are the norm. Churches of all faiths need to adapt to the times or risk becoming obsolete.

At the national level, the Unitarian Universalist Association inadvertently looks to the past by placing a priority on issues and causes above congregational health and vitality. (More about this in chapter five.) The Association has recently has taken positions in favor of clean air and against the federal government's policy on drugs. While these are worthy causes, they are secular issues of an immense scale, vastly beyond the movement's resources to change for the better in some important way. The Association has a history of taking on issues of great magnitude. Invariably, these efforts are ineffective and short-lived, yet we laud ourselves with self-congratulation for our efforts in "justice making."

Another factor to be reckoned with is that over the past ten to fifteen years, membership in UU churches has remained flat, despite UU publications that claim the Association is stronger than ever and that, "We're growing!" (Numerical growth has actually occurred in only about fifty to sixty congregations of 1,008 in the Association.) The year 2003 brought a decrease in adult membership and a second consecutive year in which the number of children and youth members declined. Is this a transitory dip, or the beginning of a long-term downward trend?

The plateau or decline of membership in UU and mainline Protestant churches stands in contrast to the sudden appearance of independent, non-denominational churches on the American religious landscape. The figures are sketchy but various reports indicate that during the past few decades, over 20,000 new churches have been founded and their adherents now total more than 15,000,000 people. One of the characteristics of newly formed churches is their ability to adapt to a rapidly changing world.

Throughout this book I'll provide examples of new churches that demonstrate this quality. For now, let me just say that I recently attended Sunday worship with about 2,500 other people at Faith Bible Chapel in Denver, Colorado. A nine-piece band of professional musicians played some outstanding music, and after the service I got a freshly brewed latte and a cranberry scone from the church café. I could have gone online at any of the six computer monitors nearby, or I could have stayed and worked out at the fully equipped gym under the direction of the church's full time athletic director.

UUs may not agree with the theology or the contemporary music of newly formed churches, but these churches display an organizational genius that enables them to grow and thrive. There is much to be learned here.

The challenge facing both local congregations and the Association today is not to reorganize committees or ponder an assortment of methods for congregational governance. The summons is to redefine Unitarian Universalism for a new era. Doing so will mean challenging long-held beliefs about what UU congregations and the larger movement should be.

Readers may find this book surprising and occasionally disconcerting. It brings to light a number of fault lines in Unitarian Universalism that are not frequently discussed. However, my intention is not to cast blame or to undermine our future, but to provide a fresh perspective for clergy and lay leaders who yearn for a more engaging church.

NOTE TO READERS: I realize that we call ourselves by many names. We are churches, congregations, societies, parishes, fellowships, and in at least one instance, a meeting. We are also Unitarian, Universalist, and Unitarian Universalist. There may be a few Universalist Unitarian churches out there, too. In this book I use the term "UU Church" and "UU Congregation" most frequently.

Also, this book is a compilation of essays, edited and placed in a sequence that provides a certain flow. Each chapter can also stand alone. Earlier versions of chapters seven, nine, and eleven were published in *Net Results* Magazine, and chapters five and eight were published in *The UU Voice*.

CHAPTER ONE

Does Your Congregation Have a Soul?

PAUL WILKES IS A RELIGION EDITOR at the *New York Times* and author of numerous books about religion in America. In his book, *Excellent Protestant Congregations*, he writes, "Religion should be a great adventure and not a leisure activity." He believes churches should be called to do things they think they cannot do, and should stick their necks out and take chances.[1]

Wilkes also writes about churches that have souls. In my work with Unitarian Universalist and mainline Protestant churches, I ask clergy and lay leaders if their churches do, indeed, have souls. Their responses, including those quoted below, are lyrical and poetic, thoughtful, provocative, and sometimes heartrending.

The quotes that follow are from clergy and lay leaders in UU churches of many sizes and from many different parts of the country. These comments will provide readers an extremely clear indication of what congregants hold in their hearts and minds, and superbly illustrate the issues that create strong and vital churches. Conversely, the comments expressed by clergy and lay leaders also point out all too clearly the issues that cause congregations to become weak and ineffective.

These comments do not require additional commentary, as they resonate powerfully on their own.

Does Your Church Have a Soul, and If So, How Would You Describe It?

"Yes. Every member of my family is better for our involvement."

"Yes, in its caring for others."

"Yes, but our church's soul is paralyzed because church leaders fear offending someone by a decision or action they may take."

"Maybe. It is in transition, at the edge of great possibilities but needs a push to get there or we may all fall backwards."

"If this church has a soul, I don't see it or feel it."

"This church has a little, wrinkled, raisin-like kernel of a soul, but with the potential to do much more to save others."

"The church's soul is not just in this building, but in the many members whose professional lives give witness to making the world a better place."

"Yes, because there is a greater presence than self."

"Yes, in theory, but only about 10 percent of us wear our souls on the outside."

"Yes, but a very conservative one. It wants badly to be 'out there' but doesn't have the courage to change."

"I see the soul of this church as analogous to that of a frustrated scholar. The theoretical knowledge of what needs to be done is there, but the will and the specific steps to address these needs are lacking."

"Yes, but it is a candidate for life support."

"Our church does not have a soul that is God-breathed."

"No soul. Too structured."

"Yes, it is in the loving acceptance of one another."

"Yes, but is hidden under the mask of protecting the status quo."

"The soul of this place is like the talent of a young artist, in need of both training and public expression."

"Like many introverted people, this church seems to hide her real self until she is called upon by extenuating circumstances."

"The soul of this church is that we value variety, and we eat well."

"A wandering soul, looking for meaning. Well intentioned but not committed."

"Yes, but it would be strengthened mightily by more intensity of focus."

"This church has more tradition than soul."

"No, and I don't think a church can have one unless people do intense work together."

"I think this church has 'flashes of soul' but we are terminally individualistic."

"Yes, but it changes quickly, and needs to be created over and over."

"Yes, but the issue is how to release it. Currently, it is stunted in its growth."

"Yes, soul is substance and core, constant as a beacon."

These comments are representative of the hundreds I've gathered over the past few years. By about a three to one margin, clergy and lay leaders yearn for churches that have more significant souls and a more powerful presence. How do we create this kind of church? Subsequent chapters address this complex question.

CHAPTER TWO

Living on Borrowed Time

IN TWENTY-FIVE YEARS, little of Unitarian Universalism as we know it may remain. Numerous church observers believe that in the coming decades, one-third or more of all churches in the United States will close their doors. Perhaps as many as 100,000 congregations will no longer exist. Among the churches closing may be 400–500 of today's 1,008 UU congregations in the United States.

Church closings stem in part from the mass exodus of people from mainline Protestant congregations that began in the late 1950s. Church closings will also result from the inability of traditional churches to recognize that seismic changes have occurred in the religious landscape around them, and their failure to respond to these changes. For example, hundreds of Universalist churches closed decades ago because their once radical message of universal salvation was absorbed into the larger culture. Having successfully preached their message, they faltered.

The disheartening scenario of church closings is a matter of demographics as well as theology. Only about fifty to sixty UU churches, 5 percent of all congregations in the Association, have seen measurable numerical growth over the past decade. The remaining 95 percent have experienced negligible growth at best; or more likely, membership plateaus and decline, as congregants grow older, grayer, and fewer.

The demographic trends also indicate that senior members, those in their seventies and eighties, the generation known as institution builders, will not be with us that much longer. This generation has supported churches with their volunteer labor for decades and decades, through good times and bad. These older members also constitute a sizeable number of the church's largest donors, through their gifts to annual pledge drives and capital campaigns. Once these dedicated souls have passed on, it is unlikely that younger generations will provide a commensurate level of financial support. Many churches will close simply because they will not have the money to remain open.

This brings us to a second demographic trend. Young people, in general, prefer large congregations because a lot more is going on. In the Association today, only forty-nine churches have 500 members or more. Three-fourths of UU congregations attract fewer than 100 people at Sunday worship, and many of those attending smaller churches are senior members. This raises the question whether younger generations will find a UU church of the size they seek. Younger people also prefer creating new forms of worship and congregational life to perpetuating the old. Since small churches place a high premium on stability and tradition, they may not be the kind of church that younger generations are looking for.

Other signs of church decline are readily apparent. Peter Wagner, author of more than twenty books about church life, summarizes what the traditional church embodies:

- **The moderate middle.** Nothing too extreme!

- **Avoiding offense.** Going to great length to avoid criticism.

- **Preserving unity.** The desire to keep everyone happy.

- **Valuing the normal.** Change is a threat to the comfort zone.

- **Gradualism.** An honored myth that the best changes go slowly.[1]

These factors, present in many UU congregations, will result in our churches drifting toward obsolescence and possibly oblivion.

Let's see how the issue of gradualism plays out in congregational life. Gradualism is the hallmark of so-called "magisterial" churches, those based on preserving a strong sense of tradition. While UU churches do not always fit this category, many behave as though they do.

For example, the newsletter in my home church illustrates gradualism perfectly. The weekly newsletter has not changed in format for over twenty years. Reading a recent issue, I had the distinct impression that I had read that newsletter before—not once but dozens of times. My church does many good things, but I was struck with the realization that we repeated the same church year over and over. I wondered if I could go back to a newsletter from about 1985, change a few names (maybe not even that many) and send it out to the congregation once again. Would parishioners even notice?

This aspect of congregational life can be referred to as, "Churches re-creating yesterday." If one church year was good, then we'll do more or less the same next year. People value the familiarity and routine that churches embody. Congregants may be reassured that in a world characterized by rapid change, the one place that remains predictable is the church. While this type of church is comforting to many, the gradualist church has not kept pace with passing times. The prominent church author Lyle Schaller wrote, "A lot of churches think next year is 1955, and plan accordingly."[2]

The most pressing issue to be addressed today is not numerical growth per se, but theological direction—whether Unitarian Universalism is a faith of the past or a faith of the future. The late Archie Epps, dean of students at Harvard University for many years once said:

> The nineteenth century was the Unitarian and the Universalist
> century, when the church claimed Emerson, Thoreau, Channing,
> Parker, Ballou, Olympia Brown, circuit-riding ministers, and nine
> consecutive Harvard presidents. The Unitarian influence has
> diminished ever since.

I take notes frequently on what clergy and lay leaders tell me about their congregations. While many churches are basically stable (though budgets always seem to be tight, and at times little more than tweaks can be made), much of what I hear is disheartening. When I ask people what they yearn for, they offer compelling responses:

"I wish my church had a more significant and visible community impact."

"I yearn for a more adventurous congregational life."

"I hope for a willingness of our church to live more boldly."

"I wish we weren't so miserly, and gave away more to meet the needs of the world."

"I wish this church took some risks. We're too comfortably settled in."

"I yearn for a church in which service is the core, and not at the edges."

"I wish we accomplished great things or affected lives."

"I wish we weren't so well established in the middle of the road."

"I yearn for a church-wide commitment to living the faith."

"I yearn for a stronger community, with less emphasis on the individual"

When I hear these yearnings I wonder why churches create vision committees that all too often devise wordy, rambling mission statements that few congregants remember, much less take to heart. The comments expressed above are powerful yearnings for what people dream their churches might become. These hopes are all the vision statements we will ever need.

These yearnings stand in contrast to four sample mission statements offered on the Association's website (**www.uua.org**) as examples for congregations to consider. The samples provided on the website each contain a service component, but that component comes last in every statement. What comes first are the following:

"We unite to provide an environment which stimulates a free exchange and exploration of ideas."

"To support each other in our various inward journeys toward truth."

"A sharing, nurturing, and caring community which promotes spiritual growth and development along with intellectual freedom."

"In joy and mutual support we offer spiritual nourishment, create beauty, affirm the worth of each individual, and honor the democratic process."

As we will discover in the next chapter, the above statements represent little that people are looking for in a church today. I hope clergy and lay leaders will return again and again to the yearnings expressed by UUs nationwide that indicate without doubt the kind of church they desire in their hearts and souls. Or, better yet, ask your fellow congregants what they, indeed, yearn for their churches to become.

Obstacles in the Pathway

When I ask church leaders what prevents them from accomplishing their hopes, dreams, and yearnings, they also have compelling responses. In my work with UU congregations, this has been a discouraging aspect of what I have found. Clergy and lay leaders say:

"We don't want to rock the boat."

"We live from crisis to crisis."

"We believe members are impoverished, and can't ask them for money."

"We don't want to offend anyone."

"There is little passion for the inherent values of the faith."

"Money is a limited resource, closely held, and carefully managed."

"People come to programs, but do not take responsibility."

"There is a sense of giving leftovers to the church."

"We are too self-absorbed and concerned about only ourselves."

"Membership is too easy here."

"We are constantly worried about running out of money and this limits any dreams we might possibly have."

"When people have good ideas in this church, the process of gaining consensus is so daunting they give up."

UU clergy and lay leaders also describe their churches as complacent, reluctant, private, cautious, ambivalent, worrisome, hesitant, sitting on their franchise, a club, anxious, stodgy, parsimonious, stingy, sterile, blasé, minimalist, uptight, afraid, living in the past, intolerant, poor, uninspired, careful, and worrisome.

Can this possibly be the UU church of the future—one that attracts new adherents?

Miroslav Volf is a theologian at Yale Divinity School, and he addresses this issue with a compelling question: "Why are communities of faith increasingly ineffective in their central task?" His answer: "Because churches do not offer a compelling vision of a way of life that is worth living." [3]

A way of life that is worth living. How simple a concept, yet how effectively do UU congregations promote and model such a vision? Unfortunately, Unitarian Universalism has succumbed to a consumer mentality. We hope members and friends like the minister's sermons, the music, the Sunday school, and our programs. If not, the church must have failed.

George Barna's surveys reveal that many people believe the ideal church is one that accommodates the individual's preferences and needs. Absent from their thinking is the church having an agenda of its own, and playing a central role in the drama.[4] I often ask clergy and lay leaders if their churches have an agenda, or a particular role or purpose in this place and time. Many have difficulty defining the church's agenda as anything beyond serving current members.

I do not wish to find fault with ministers for the state of the Unitarian Universalist faith today. Nevertheless, William Murry, former president of Meadville Lombard Theological School in Chicago, stated his concerns powerfully in a sermon at the installation of a newly settled minister:

> Perhaps the ministry itself has been partially responsible for its
> loss of status and respect . . . Too often we have understood our
> task as relegated to the private sphere, the personal lives of our

members. We have encouraged and facilitated their turn from a religion of love and justice to a religion of personal spirituality. Too often we have been content simply to help people feel better about themselves, without challenging their self-centeredness.

Too often we have preached sermons on trivial and inconsequential subjects rather than address the significant issues of our time. In a word, too many of our ministers and churches have retreated into the safety and security of the private sphere and have little or no public ministry, and that is tragic. The result is the liberal church and its ministers are seen today as largely irrelevant to the workings of the real world. The church and its ministry have been relegated to the backwaters of society, and too many of us have accepted that place without objection or rebellion.[5]

What is to be done?

Redefining What It Means to Be a Unitarian Universalist

Unitarian Universalism is reaping an unfortunate harvest of a low expectation faith. Low, ambiguous, or almost non-existent expectations of membership exist in many congregations. It is not uncommon for membership literature of UU congregations to contain the phrase, "To participate in the many programs and activities of the church, you do not need to be a member." Here lies the starting point for a renewed religious movement.

Rather than continue the tradition of asking people for little when they join a church, we should explore the concept of "integrity of membership." For too long we have allowed people to pledge $50 or $100 (or nothing!) attend worship on Christmas and Easter (if then!) yet feel obligated to bend to their needs, whims, complaints, and demands, as they expect a full service church to address their every concern.

As a needed alternative, integrity of membership begins with regular attendance at Sunday worship. Today, most UU churches attract less than half the membership to Sunday services. A Baptist friend of mine says, "You don't call your boss and tell him you're sleeping in, and you don't do that with God, either!" UU minister

Victor Carpenter often said, "Small miracles occur at church every Sunday" and he is right. People need to worship together regularly. Unitarian Universalism should not be a "fair weather" faith, one in which we come to church only when it is convenient, or when an interesting topic will be addressed.

This brings to mind a story about William Ellery Channing, minister of the Federal Street Church (now the Arlington Street Church) in Boston in the 1850s. While walking to church one Sunday morning, Channing encountered a parishioner. Channing greeted the man and suggested they continue together to worship. The parishioner replied that he didn't care for the sermon topic that day and would not be in attendance. From that time forward, Channing never again announced the Sunday sermon title or topic.

I recommend that churches today discontinue the practice of placing the sermon topic, title, and speaker in the newsletter. This encourages congregants to develop a "pick and choose faith." They like this topic, so they'll be there. They don't like that one, so they'll stay home. For venturesome clergy who wish to remove the sermon title from the newsletter and encounter the refrain, "We've never done that before," or, "I have the right to choose the sermons I want to hear," the Channing example is the ideal precedent, dating back more than 150 years!

The Authentic Church

Church literature today points out that "church shoppers" are on self-identified religious pilgrimages. They are seeking an "authentic" community of faith. What does this mean, and how do we create such a congregation?

To create an authentic church will require a conviction in our hearts and minds that Unitarian Universalism can change people's lives for the better in some fundamental way. I suspect many UUs, clergy included, don't conceive of our churches having the power to do this. Or, perhaps more significantly, we don't think that changing lives is the church's business.

For example, in reading through newsletters from numerous UU churches, I selected a representative sample of current programs: dream study, drumming circles, a gardening group, an investors group, a quilting group, a class on writing your memoirs, a class on writing non-fiction articles, a class on learning sign language, a potluck with the screening of a film about the Spanish writer Federico Garcia Lorca, and finally—a class on UU heritage. Even this lone UU program is geared toward the past and not the future.

The issue is not whether churches should present programs, as a certain level of programming is a good thing. The issue is whether the church should focus primarily on secular topics that are equally appropriate for adult education centers. Programs gather people together, but what do these subjects have to do with living a spiritual life, or creating a more just and humane world? I recall a Lutheran minister saying that the purpose of a church is not to bring people into the building and "cage" them in programs. The major purpose of a church is to empower people to go out and make the world a better place in which to live.

The content of many church programs reflects the concern in William Murry's sermon excerpt that the spiritual life in UU churches is often viewed as an inward process of self-enlightenment rather than a commitment to a community of faith.

Episcopal Bishop John Shelby Spong addresses this very topic in his book, *Why Christianity Must Change or Die*. He writes:

> Love is the source and creator of life. Love is the essential power that deepens our relationships and simultaneously expands our humanity. The more we are freed to be ourselves, the more we are enabled to give our lives away to others. The more we know of life-giving love, the more we find the courage to express and reveal the ground of our being.[6]

Spong's view reflects the simple yet powerful prayer of John Wesley, founder of Methodism, "That I may become master of myself so I can be a servant to others."

These voices stand in contrast to a common Unitarian Universalist message that a life of faith is an inner process of self-discovery.

A steady diet of programs and social events allows congregants to be observers rather than participants in the ministry of the church.

Church programs also tend to be based on accumulating information rather changing people's lives. The congregation of the future is one that will recognize the unique ability of the church to radically alter a person's worldview, and help people realize they are no longer the people they had once been. Too often we view UU churches as safe havens, places of comfort that are perceived as a final destination rather than a port of embarkation.

Anthony Robinson, a minister of the United Church of Christ, addressed this issue in his book, *Transforming Congregational Culture.*[7] Robinson writes that when in the pulpit, he often felt like an op-ed columnist, commenting on events of the times, throwing in an anecdote or two, a bit of Scripture, and some pearls of wisdom for people to live by. He felt his role was to enlighten and entertain the congregation on Sunday mornings. He writes that he came away from the experience with an ache in his heart that he thought would never heal.

Robinson felt this way until he read an article by poet Annie Dillard who said that when people come to church they should not be handed an order of service with a smile, but should be given hard hats and life preservers; because church should be a dangerous place, a zone of risk, a place of new birth and new life, where we confront ourselves with who we truly are and who the church is calling us to become.

These are the elements of an authentic community of faith. If we do not believe the church embodies a higher calling and the power to change people's lives, then where do we go from here?

Charitable Giving Should Be Fun, Shouldn't It?

Next in redefining Unitarian Universalism, we must confront head-on the disgraceful pattern of low-level giving. In most UU churches, 50 to 60 percent of congregants pledge less than $10 per week. Clergy and lay leaders across the land report that the culture of money in their congregations is one of scarcity, even in affluent communities and in churches with sizable assets. A constant struggle for money is too often the norm.

In my work with congregations I talk about tithing! (For UUs who protest they are atheists or humanists and do not relate to the biblical concept of tithing, I recommend 11 percent, a figure that has no religious meaning whatsoever.) I know many UUs who came from mainline Protestant families that tithed, and who continue this tradition today. These generous souls often have fond remembrances from childhood of putting a nickel or dime into a small envelope, and placing that envelope in the offering plate as it was passed around at Sunday worship. The concept of giving to the church in good measure was a family affair, with parents setting the example.

In this era, churches should help people of all generations lead lives that cut across the grain of the consumer-oriented society. UU minister Beth Banks believes that churches must emphasize this element of family life, otherwise, "We cheat ourselves and our children from having lives of meaning and purpose, and invite in cynicism and helplessness." We must renew the importance of charitable giving among people of all ages, as a core value of people of faith. This does not mean asking people for more money to pay the church's bills. The challenge is to redefine the "good life," as one that goes beyond acquiring ever more consumer goods.

Robert Wuthnow is Director of the Center for the Study of American Religion at Princeton University, and he often writes about the proverbial good life. He notes that we may decry the gross materialism of the times, but this might not change our own desire for additional wealth.[8] Anthony Robinson addresses this issue in a more expansive and deeply religious context: "People need relationships in which they experience love—to detoxify from a culture that is toxic in its materialism, individualism, and violence and move toward whole new lives, new attitudes, new relationships, new perspectives."[9]

Church consultant Thomas Bandy also speaks of the good life in his lectures. One of his "traveling necessities" that churches should carry with them is the belief that anyone can lead a life that is equal to, or better than, the affluent. Churches need to challenge the prevailing consumerism that shouts from every vantage point that we do not have enough, and that people who have less are relegated to an inferior status.

UU churches should challenge their members and friends to lead lives of dedication, commitment, and even sacrifice. This is the good life. But this is not work for the faint of heart. Living a life of faith is not always easy, and in fact, should not be.

Finally, What Are We Doing with It?

A. Powell Davies was the senior minister of All Souls Church in Washington, D.C., after World War II. Davies, a powerful orator, was the founder of thirteen churches in the area. In a sermon he once preached:

> Do you belong to a religion that says humankind is not divided—
> except by ignorance and prejudice and hate; the religion that sees
> humankind as naturally one and waiting to be spiritually united; the
> religion that proclaims an end to all exclusions—and declares a
> brotherhood and sisterhood unbounded! The religion that knows we
> shall never find the fullness of the wonder and the glory of life until
> we are ready to share it, that we shall never have hearts big enough
> for the love of God until we have made them big enough for the
> worldwide love of one another.
>
> As you have listened to me, have you thought perchance that
> this is your religion? If so, do not congratulate yourself. Stop long
> enough to recollect the miseries of the world in which you live;
> the fearful cruelties, the enmities, the hate, the bitter prejudices,
> the need of such a world for such a faith. And if you can still say
> that this of which I have spoken is your faith, then ask yourself this
> question: What are you doing with it? [10]

Davies raised this question in the 1950s and it is even more urgent today. What are we doing with our faith? Not nearly enough. Most UU churches serve educated, middle class, relatively affluent white people. Is this our only calling? I yearn for the day that our churches will boldly reclaim a heritage of faithfulness and service. We must do this to survive as a religious movement.

CHAPTER THREE

A Church
of the 1950s?

NTHONY ROBINSON, a minister in the United Church of Christ has done UU clergy and lay leaders a big favor by writing a book titled, *Transforming Congregational Culture*.[1]

Robinson tells of a small town of the 1950s in Washington State that conducted a contest to identify the town's "Best Christian." Residents cast their ballots for the person they believed most worthy of the award. As irony would have it, the town's only Jewish resident was the winner! This man was described as kind, helpful, and an asset to the community. Theology played little role in the scheme of things.

With this story Robinson demonstrates the dynamics of what he calls, "civic faith." During the 1950s the country reflected a predominantly Christian ethos. Churchgoers were expected to be good people, solid citizens, loyal Americans, and committed parents. Newcomers were also assumed to embody these traits, and it was generally accepted that newcomers were already "believers," as well.

In this scenario, people who joined the church were provided a brief orientation, placed on church committees, and congregational life continued as before. The "modern" Protestant church of the 1950s was based on reason, an emphasis on the individual, human self-sufficiency, optimism, and a belief in progress. (UU readers will find these traits familiar.)

Theologian Reinhold Niebuhr raised concern that churches should challenge the secular society rather than being accommodated by it, but his voice and others did not gain a foothold in churches at that time.

The civic faith worked until about 1960, when people began leaving mainline churches in droves. Many felt that if church was little more than a reflection of secular society, who needed it? Those who stayed tended to maintain the civic faith, the only one they had ever known.

A Different World Order

Today, in a society marked by religious pluralism, Robinson believes people are seeking a church for very different reasons. In his experience of twenty-five years as a minister, he has found the leading edge questions that bring people to church now are:

- How can I lead a deeper spiritual life?
- How can I be engaged with something beyond day-to-day secular life?
- How can I be part of a community of meaning and purpose?

People coming to churches today are often motivated by crises in their lives; or they are seeking change, transformation, a life that is fundamentally different, or one that is deeper in meaning. In the face of such motivations, theological distinctions matter little.

Robinson contends that the civic faith, with its reliance on reason, freedom, and individual autonomy do not answer the questions people have today. He writes, "I had been prepared by background and education for a church and a world that were vanishing."[2]

Theologian Walter Brueggemann captured this aspect of changing congregational life perfectly: "The church that you have been preparing so carefully is being taken away from you—by the grace of God."[3]

"Can churches deliver the goods and create more compelling communities of faith?" Robinson asks. He believes such an outcome is possible if: we view church not as a place for accumulating information but as a process of forming a people; if the church engages not the intellect alone, but the whole person; and instead of reflecting the consumer society, churches provide members an alternative way of life.

So, gentle readers, do we have a faith and a message that has changed to meet the challenges of the day, or have we remained in the 1950s?

CHAPTER FOUR

Criteria for Successful Churches

OVER THE PAST FEW YEARS I've served as a consultant to twenty-three UU churches in the United States and Canada, ranging in size from 315 to 1,350 members. Consultants would like to believe they can assist any potential client who calls, and for a while I succumbed to this desire to be helpful. Consequently, I worked with a few churches that I wished I hadn't. These churches were entrenched in a way of congregational life that was unlikely to change despite their pressing problems and my best efforts.

Experienced consultants have a keen awareness that the so-called "presenting problem" a congregation puts forward is often not the real issue. This state of affairs has probably become evident to ministers in search who meet with search committees. People who serve on search committees are extremely thoughtful and want to do a good job, but congregational surveys and the findings of focus groups about the qualities that members want in a minister may not be entirely accurate. Congregants do not always want what they claim they want.

In particular, church leaders often declare that they want change. However, barring a perceived crisis, many congregations will drift along with the status quo, more or less aimlessly. Indeed, church leaders may resist change mightily. This observation is not a criticism of anyone in particular, but rather an acknowledgement that for many people, church is a stable part of life. People enjoy the predictability of the church year, with its holidays, holy days, and familiar rhythms. They take comfort in the Order of Service and in singing hymns they know well. Many people don't want to come to church and find the routine all changed around, especially by younger members who "don't know how we do things around here."

As a parish consultant I have learned that a "status quo" church is not one I can work with productively. Thus, I established a set of criteria that I ask clergy and lay leaders to review before we do any work together. If a church does not meet these criteria, it is unlikely I will be able to assist them. Church leaders have also told me of intense discussions over whether their church meets these criteria.

These criteria are:

- A willingness among church leaders to keep open minds in reviewing current patterns of congregational life, and a willingness to consider different methods if they hold promise.

- A willingness of church leaders not to have the keenest minds focused only on institutional maintenance of the church (administration, finance, and property) but on outreach efforts, as well.

- An attitude among clergy and lay leaders that money is an instrument to accomplish much good in the world, not a "necessary evil." The annual pledge drive needs to be viewed as an essential ministry of the church, not the tedious task of asking people for money.

- A willingness to clarify and, most likely, raise the expectations of membership, including the expectation of charitable giving in good measure.

- A willingness of church leaders to discuss charitable giving as a core element of being people of faith, and to set an example for parishioners in their own giving.

- A willingness to challenge the attitude of scarcity often found in UU churches, along with dispelling the myth that many congregants are poor and can give only a pittance to the church. (Lyle Schaller's "line of demarcation" between churches that will thrive and those that will not is based on this very concept—an attitude of abundance or an attitude of scarcity, as each becomes a self-fulfilling prophecy.)[1]

- ❧ A willingness of church leaders to consider the "permission granting" model of congregational life that encourages people to begin compassionate outreach efforts when they encounter unhappiness in the world around them. This includes a willingness to fund new initiatives and not let a, "We don't have the money" attitude prevail.

- ❧ A willingness of the church to allocate 10 percent of the operating budget for outreach. This allocation is in addition to Association and District dues.

- ❧ And finally, a willingness of church leaders to lead—to make decisions without taking surveys "to see what people think" before instituting new policies. In most churches, 50 percent or more of members are relatively inert, and it is not necessary to gain a majority vote of the congregation as a whole.

Might your church meet these criteria? I believe these principles are necessary for UU churches to create a viable future.

CHAPTER FIVE

Making Manual Typewriters

I ONCE READ THAT WELL INTO THE 1980s, the former Soviet Union was the world's leading manufacturer of manual typewriters. When I observe how we go about church life today, I wonder if we are using the equivalent of manual typewriters and carbon paper when a higher level of technology is readily available to us.

Episcopal priest Philip Wiehe wrote, "Over the past two thousand years we have developed an enormous amount of church procedure, some of which we zealously retain."[1] We may discard certain practices on occasion, but some church methods today date back to the Colonial era and have outlived their usefulness.

At times, it also appears that we model churches after the federal government. For example, the Presbyterian Church (U.S.A.) has an operating budget of $135 million, 173 Presbyteries (comparable to our twenty districts), and sixteen regional Synods. A number of staff people who work for the PCUSA told me that routine matters become extremely complicated, given the multitude of committees, task forces, study groups, and advisory boards. A minority of these bodies addresses issues involving effective local congregations. Like the UUA, the Presbyterian denomination places a priority on issues and causes rather than on congregational strength and vitality. (By the way, the PCUSA and its predecessor bodies have lost more than 35,000 adult members each year for the past forty years.)

Let's take a moment to examine the matter of denominations focusing on issues and causes rather than creating and sustaining strong congregations. In a recent article, Dale Bullard, director of the Hollifield Learning Center in North Carolina wrote:

> The following are two issues for which denominations must accept responsibility. First, some denominations lost their way a couple of generations ago when they determined that their role revolved around causes and issues rather than congregational vitality and new church starts. After a strong generation of starting new churches following World War II, it seemed like a natural step for churches to address the massive social changes and urban crises of the 1960s.
>
> An equally challenging issue is that seminaries *[during these years]* graduated many ministers who focused on issues and causes. As a result, a whole generation or so of ministry leaders forgot how to do evangelism, new-member recruitment, and church planting.
>
> Furthermore, some denominations took what they perceived to be prophetic stands on justice issues. A few denominations continue this practice. While this pattern may be perceived as right for many reasons, a by-product is that church members often do not share these views and feel their spiritual needs are going unmet.
>
> Second, when the cutting-edge agenda of ministry changed at the grassroots and called for a focus on new congregations, church vitality, and church planting, denominations responded slowly. Rather than taking a leadership role for the next stage of church development, many denominations lagged behind.
>
> Before denominations could respond to the new agenda, they found themselves as objects of a post-denominational era. They embroiled themselves in internal struggles between special interest groups with opposing ideologies and struggled for their financial viability, especially as traditional funding streams began to plateau or diminish. Into this void have rushed many highly successful independent congregations that have little or no denominational affiliation, as well as eager parachurch organizations that could respond more quickly than many denominations did.[2]

Bullard correctly identifies our Association as one with a priority on issues and causes rather than congregational health and vitality.

For example, the Association has embraced many causes over the past forty-three years. As of this writing, the agenda of this year's General Assembly includes: marriage equality, oppression of women worldwide, stopping mass extinction, global warming, and reform of the criminal justice and prison systems. An impressive list, but does anyone remember what the issues were at last year's General Assembly? Or the General Assembly before that? General Assembly, the delegate body that represents the interests of congregations, has devolved into a traveling Chautauqua, selecting multiple causes and issues that receive little attention after everyone has gone home. Were any of these issues acted upon to any significant degree in UU congregation across the nation?

No doubt we support worthy causes, but established groups deal with secular issues far more effectively. If we wish to further secular causes, we can do considerably better than attempting to replicate existing organizations on a miniscule scale.

We have fallen into the habit of viewing the Association's primary role as introducing new initiatives that congregations should support, rather than the Association's major focus as supporting churches across the land.

An emphasis on issues and causes also adds to the shortage of leadership in religious institutions. For example, in 1996 *Christianity Today* magazine listed fifty "up and coming" religious leaders under the age of forty. Of the fifty, only six worked in parish or denominational settings. Many of the remaining forty-four claimed their creativity would be unacceptably stifled in such organizations. They believed the message of the established church was ambiguous and misguided, and that when people are mired in organizational structures, usually committees, their vision is deadened.

The Basic Church Model?

Let's take a look at the way many UU churches function, based on a business or non-profit model. We'll pretend that we want to start a new business or a non-profit organization, and are formulating a plan for success.

First, we decide to hire people who are independent minded, who will be skeptical and perhaps resistant to our leadership and authority. We might also require that a certain percentage are people who whine and complain when they don't get their way. Upon hiring these new employees, we will convey low expectations of them. We will then price our product or service so low that it creates a climate of almost perpetual financial anxiety. This, in turn, means we will pay employees the absolute minimum. If this formula does not succeed, we will keep cutting back until it does.

Of course this is preposterous, but in actuality is how many UU congregations function. This approach is a liability that has become embedded in Unitarian Universalism's "genetic code," and few churches are immune from its influence.

The New Church

The institutional baggage of the established church has not gone unnoticed by younger generations of church leaders. Sociologist Donald Miller, author of the thought-provoking book, *Reinventing American Protestantism*, writes, "The untold story of American Protestantism today is the growth and proliferation of independent churches."[3] He likens the era in which we live to the Second Great Awakening of 1800–30, a time when established religions were challenged by upstart preachers and evangelists.

The appearance of new churches includes a prevously unseen species in American religion, the independent, non-denominational "mega-church," with 10,000 members or more. Traditional faiths attempt to ignore newly formed churches, mainly because leaders of these churches abandoned long ago the hope that established denominations could be reformed. Instead, a cadre of venturesome souls went out and created a new order of church.

Miller writes:

For many observers, the newly formed church defies common
sense. Why would churches characterized by tolerance, rationality,
and scientific sophistication be declining while those that are
morally strict, theologically intolerant, and emotionally expressive
in their worship be growing?[4]

Miller also suggests that people in traditional churches would like
to pay no heed to this revolution in American religion. He writes:

The typical defense is to label these groups as fundamentalist reac-
tionaries. But such dismissals ignore the complexity of these
movements. They are not socially marginal. Quite the contrary,
they are middle-class churches that represent the mainstream of
American society. While conservative theologically, many are relatively avant-garde culturally— much more so than the typical
mainline congregation—and they are far from being socially re-
gressive. To outsiders, they often look conservative as they affirm
traditional roles for women, demonstrate against abortion, and
bash contemporary psychology. But this is not fundamentalism
resurrected. Gone is the authoritarianism associated with that tradition, and absent is fundamentalism's opposition to modernity;
the belief that a return to a bygone era will solve the perceived
chaos of the present.[5]

These new churches are something that UUs need to learn more
about. Criticism of conservative churches from liberals is often ineffective because it tends to be poorly informed, misguided, and
defensive.

Many newly founded churches sound like miracle stories. Miller
tells the story of a young man with a high school education who was
called to ministry. With little seminary training and a moderate
amount of church experience, he moved from Southern California
to Albuquerque, rented a vacant storefront, and started a new
church. That church ultimately grew to over 10,000 members.

This story, on a smaller scale of success, has been repeated thousands of times over the past few decades in the United States and
around the world. Some churches in Africa and Latin America have

attracted hundreds of thousands of members. There is no denominational structure to "support" these churches.

Who's in Charge Overall?

Returning to the Presbyterians for a moment, author Peter Wagner also reported:

> In 1992 someone raised the question of what the vision of the denomination might be. Because of established church polity, no one in the organization could be trusted to give that answer. So, the decision was made to convene a church council, with a mandate to identify the priorities of the church.

Wagner continues:

> The result was a 256-page document, detailing 143 priorities! When no one can cast a vision, the vision becomes so diffuse that it is next to meaningless. Most new-church leaders would have a difficult time believing a council [like this] would ever take place.[6]

Who's in Charge at the Church?

In UU polity, despite the language of "call," ministers are typically viewed as employees of the church. Therefore, the locus of decision-making is frequently not the minister, but the board, various committees, and other bodies in the church. Mainline Protestant church bodies adhere to a similar structure. We claim to heed prophetic voices and say that individuals are worthy of dignity and trust, but in practice we believe that decisions made by committees are safer. Our churches certainly don't want any "loose cannons" out there unless one or more committees have approved their ideas in advance.

But decisions made by groups also present risks. The 1997 report by the UUA's Commission on Appraisal titled, "Interdependence: Renewing Congregational Polity," raised this very issue. The Commission reported, "If the only way that minority groups can get the attention of the majority is to act in ways that are dramatic, if not bizarre to some people, then some aspect of our system of governance is failing."[7]

The Commission identified a symptom of failure, but not the cause. Partly because our congregations have low expectations of membership, as many as two-thirds of members can be defined as observers rather than participants in the ministry of the church. Because of misguided notions of congregational polity, clergy and lay leaders often feel an obligation to include inactive members (an oxymoron) in congregational votes, surveys, and various decisions. The tradition of congregational polity has come to mean (erroneously) that all who come will be heard and served in equal measure.

The value we assign to, "The inherent worth and dignity of each individual" also suggests that whatever anyone has to say warrants consideration. This postmodern view equates equal value to opinions that people hold. At times, we act as though uninformed opinions are as valuable as informed opinions.

The upshot is that sometimes people come to churches (of all faiths) with opinions, views, and expectations that cannot possibly be addressed. Instead of saying, "We don't do that here," church leaders feel an obligation to consider all views and provide fair hearings. As a result, clergy and lay leaders often find themselves swept up in people's personal agendas rather than the larger mission of the church.

How many times have we heard of UU churches in conflict, with arguments among the deists, theists, humanists, atheists, agnostics, Christians, pagans, and a plethora of other interest groups; all wishing to have their points of view upheld, with some unyielding in their views? These are churches that attempt to serve members' needs. Such congregations are unable to move forward toward a larger purpose for being.

The Commission on Appraisal is correct that our system of governance is failing. The reality is that an emphasis on equality, diversity of belief, the democratic process, and misunderstood congregational polity has hastened that failure.

With so many voices to be heard, the potential for internal dissent becomes more likely, and the leadership of congregations and the Association is weakened. Ministers and lay leaders are unable to act as leaders and are forced into being enablers, facilitators, mediators, and caretakers. Like the Presbyterians, we end up with 143 priorities—all too often issues and agendas that people bring to church—rather than a clear and informed vision of what creates congregations of health, vitality, meaning, and purpose.

Leaders Should Lead!

Strong leadership is the core issue that distinguishes newly formed independent congregations from established churches. These new churches include nondenominational communities that attract large numbers of people in their twenties and thirties. (People in established churches tend to believe that young people will not get up early on Sunday morning to go to church, but in fact they do.)

A prevailing belief in newly formed churches is that the sheep do not lead the shepherd. Nor do the sheep discipline the shepherd, by means of performance reviews or congregational surveys. The minister is called to lead, and expected to lead.

UU's are highly unlikely to allow a minister this degree of authority and influence. But I believe we should empower clergy, not make them a vehicle for our prevailing views, thoughts, opinions, and sometimes prejudices. A mistaken definition of congregational polity has created a system in which lay leaders, often well intentioned but woefully unprepared for their roles by a lack of orientation and training, make (or fail to make) decisions based on little more than instinct. This system places authority in the hands of people who may know the least about the nature and character of churches, and who withhold permission from ministers and talented lay leaders who may know the most. UUs may claim to be anti-establishment rebels, but in fact many of our congregations embody established church behavior.

For example, in my work with churches I frequently ask, "What happens when someone has a really great idea, one that might cost $1,000?" More often than not, one or more committees have to approve any new idea, and the finance committee or board has to approve any new expenditure. Such a process can take months. This system creates "authority-less" people at many levels who find themselves withholding permission for new initiatives, often proposed by the most enthusiastic and talented members of the church.

Loren Mead, an Episcopal priest and founder of the Alban Institute, writes about this aspect of congregational life in his book, *More Than Numbers: The Ways Churches Grow.* He refers to a type of "organic" growth, in which congregational leaders realized their structures were obstacles to new initiatives rather than pathways, and made it considerably easier for people to initiate new ideas.[8] This is the church of the future.

I recall saying to the Senior Minister of a UU church of 650 members that I thought a dozen people could manage the church just fine. He replied:

> No, you're wrong. It would take only about half a dozen. Instead, I have 250 people on thirty-seven committees, and this unnecessary bureaucracy creates an inward focus, diminishes our larger mission, and forces people to invest their time and energy in issues that don't really matter very much.

Is There Hope?

Today, people have powerful problems and seek a powerful faith. We have the talent and the financial means to create such a church. However, the jury is still out on whether we will empower clergy and lay people to lead us in this direction.

The Alban Institute, an organization that studies church life, released a report titled, *The Leadership Situation Facing American Congregations.* Overall, its conclusions were distressing, including:

> Theological students increasingly indicate a reluctance to serve in congregational settings. They cite several common concerns: the job is simply unmanageable; boundaries between personal and professional time cannot be established; the variety of roles they must fill creates unreasonable expectations and confusing standards; and an absence of effective models of decision making, communication, and leadership hinders their work.[9]

Surprisingly, the Alban Institute concluded, "The system is fundamentally healthy enough to put up a fight." I question whether this was wishful thinking.

UU churches need to examine their existing congregational structures carefully to determine whether they indeed function as a foundation for tomorrow's church. The question at hand is whether we limit the effectiveness of capable clergy, lay leaders, and church members via outdated practices, policies, and structures.

My colleague Thomas Bandy often asks whether we help clergy, lay leaders, and people in the pews become gifted and able to hear the call to fulfill the mission of the church? Or, are people supervised and kept, by overlapping committees and policies that thwart imagination and keep people in their places?

Historian David McCullough writes his books on a 1942 Royal manual typewriter, but he's an exception. Churches cannot live in 1942. UU congregations should be in the business of empowering ministers and lay leaders to reach out and serve when opportunities arise; and take risks when necessary, so our churches can become engaged in the larger world in ever-greater ways. Churches seldom die from taking risks. They expire from becoming complacent. A friend of mine recently said, "Religion requires guts!" Churches with fortitude are the churches of the future.

CHAPTER SIX

Parishioners
as Consumers

Do you remember the church-shopping couple in the *Doonesbury* comic strip? They had their list. When they met with cartoon character Rev. Scott Sloane (modeled after William Sloane Coffin and UU minister Scotty McLennan) they asked, "Does the church serve cappuccino at coffee hour? Is there volleyball on Tuesday evenings? No? Well, the Episcopalians down the street offer a better deal."

People today are sometimes viewed as coming to church with a consumer attitude, one of "what's in it for me?" All too often, UU and mainline Protestant churches play this losing game. To their detriment, churches inadvertently convey the message, "We hope you like us." If not, the church must have failed, by not meeting your needs.

The membership pamphlet of a large UU church contains the phrase, "The professional staff is here to meet your needs." This way of thinking is a great weakness of the contemporary UU church. The purpose of a church is not to serve middle class people, many who already enjoy a multitude of life's privileges. The purpose of a church is to call people to serve. Sadly, a number of UU ministers have told me they believe their primary role is to keep parishioners satisfied.

George Barna's surveys find that an increasing number of Americans perceive the church as a "rest stop" along their spiritual journeys rather than a final destination. People seem to believe that spirituality is a discovery process of enlightenment and not a commitment to a faith group or perspective. They believe religion is a commodity to be consumed, not one in which to invest. Matters of faith are a take-only, and not a give-and-take proposition.[1]

Unitarian Universalism does not face this issue alone. No organization in America today has lost as much moral authority and as many adherents as the traditional church. Thomas Bandy often says, "Many churches motivate people to go home and have lunch."

Unitarian Universalism has a proud history and tradition, one with its saints and martyrs. But what are our churches called to do in this place and time? The primary purpose of the church is to create a community of compassion. All else flows from this. UU churches should call their members to lead lives of dedication and commitment—lives not just of success, but also of service, and when called upon, sacrifice.

In the 1920s theologian Karl Barth wrote, "When people come to church, they consciously or unconsciously leave behind them cherry tree, symphony, state, daily work, and other things, as possibilities somehow exhausted."[2] At church, Barth declared, people seek a new and infinitely greater possibility. Today, however, many people leave the church behind; and seek spirituality in that very same cherry tree, symphony, state, daily work, and everyday life.

In fact, UU churches often encourage congregants away from lives of faithfulness in community. Don't want to come to church on Sunday? Well, a walk on the beach or in the woods is just as good. At times Unitarian Universalism has come to embody the belief that spirituality is found in so many places that the church is just one among many, with no greater or lesser value. To be sure, the natural world can be radiant with beauty and restore a weary soul. But to worship together effectively, congregants must do something else, as well. Being appreciative of the forest or the beach, or going to the symphony, however, are not sufficient to be that "something else."

Carl Scovel, minister emeritus of King's Chapel in Boston, often says that Unitarian Universalism is a kind of institutionalized transcendentalism. We wish to build community, but we emphasize individuality to a degree that at times borders on the obsessive. This creates a church of two minds, and fosters the attitude that people expect the church to meet their needs primarily.

Silvio Nardoni, a UU minister and attorney in Southern California, challenges this consumer sentiment with a metaphorical example of windows. Does your church have clear glass windows, through which the congregation looks out onto a world in which sorrow and unhappiness are all too evident? Or are those windows more like mirrors, reflecting only the comfort, convenience, and needs of parishioners inside? To continue this metaphor from the outside, can people passing by see in through those windows, or are those windows opaque to an outsider's point of view?

Unitarian Universalism should be creating churches that make the world a more just, safe, and equitable place. This goal will not be accomplished if church leaders believe their primary role is to accommodate the people who are already there. I have made the recommendation to numerous congregations that they discontinue the annual "satisfaction" surveys. UU churches should get out of the satisfaction business. More important issues are at stake.

CHAPTER SEVEN

WJST:
Would Jesus Say That?

A S A CHURCH consultant I assist UU and mainline Protestant congregations with issues of church health and vitality. By far, the most problematic area of my work with clergy and lay leaders is the meaning of membership.

Listed below are quotes from the membership literature of numerous UU churches. Would Jesus have said, "Come, follow me . . ."

But you may not be a joiner.

Even if you only come on Sunday morning.

But you don't need to make a commitment.

Whenever you wish.

If you haven't gotten around to it yet.

And we will respect your anonymity.

But you don't need to become a member.

And let us know when you leave, so we don't have to pay per-head Association dues.

It is impossible to imagine that Jesus, or any other effective religious leader, would be so lukewarm in calling people to follow. Yet in my experience, that tepid tone is the norm in UU churches.

Peter Wagner writes, "The current revolution is not so much against apostasy, but against irrelevance." [1] People come to church seeking sustenance, but they often find a diluted version of the message. Would Jesus have used this language? I don't think so.

CHAPTER EIGHT

A Religious Movement in Decline?

THE EVIDENCE IS UNMISTAKABLE. Unitarian Universalism appears to be in a slow and inexorable decline. My intention is not to find fault with any particular person or group for bringing this situation about. Rather, I believe the world is passing us by, and we haven't noticed.

Let me summarize the reasons we have arrived at this place. Along with this dire analysis, I offer some hopeful strategies that might reverse the downward spiral in which the movement finds itself.

Over the past decade or so, annual growth in membership in UU churches has been about 0.8 percent. *That is not 8 percent; it is eight-tenths of 1 percent.* This percentage translates into about 900 new members in the 1,008 congregations in the United States, less than one new member per congregation. The growth rate of 8.8 percent since 1994 (0.8 percent per year times ten years), seemingly impressive on the surface, paints an erroneous portrait of membership. This growth rate is barely more than that one new member per congregation per year. (It bears repeating that only about fifty or sixty churches out of 1,008 have shown numerical growth over the past decade.)

As the population of the country has increased, UU's also constitute a smaller percentage of the population as a whole. At best, our faith is in a holding pattern as people in the pews grow older and grayer. More likely, ours is a movement in decline.

The claim of "significant growth opportunities," found in UUA District plans are correct that the climate exists for increased membership. The quest for spirituality has long been underway; and the sales of books, seminars, and other spirituality-based programs are at record levels. People are more willing than ever to cross denominational boundaries to find an elusive spirituality. They are more willing to explore multiple sources to find religious meaning. These people sound like us! Shouldn't they be coming to UU churches?

Unfortunately, the policies, practices, and approaches we use as congregations and as an Association will inadvertently encourage these potential new members to pass us by.

Many factors contribute to this decline, and some are forces beyond our control. Millions of people have abandoned mainline Protestant traditions, mostly middle class churchgoers who closely resemble UUs. Also, in decades past, the prevailing expectation was that a family attended church together. With many divorced households today, it is increasingly unlikely that both parents will take their children to church. UU ministers also report a decreasing number of men attending Sunday worship.

Yet another factor is that significant numbers of people believe they will not find spirituality within organized religion. They believe they can create their own personal faith, if they have any interest in the subject at all.

Additional factors are of our own making. Prominent among them is our unwillingness to look outside our own boundaries for phenomena that have had a detrimental impact on UU churches, fellowships, and the movement as a whole. For example, we rail against the rise of conservative churches rather than trying to understand whey they are so successful. We discount the validity of these churches, thinking their members, even highly educated professionals, have been hoodwinked or led astray. Perhaps worst of all, we claim that significant shifts in the religious world do not apply to us because we are "different" or "unique."

Church-growth expert Lyle Schaller describes this phenomenon accurately. He writes, "Some denominations function with a playbook that was last revised in the 1950s, and are unwilling to write a new playbook for a new game."[1] Schaller points out numerous tactics that undermine the health and vitality of traditional faiths. I have chosen a few that are particularly relevant to UU churches, districts, and the Association. They include:

- Let highly divisive social, political, and secular issues dominate the agenda at the annual meeting of the denomination. These include issues such as vouchers for school children, government policies, and various gradations of political correctness.
- Foster small-church policies that do not serve large congregations.
- Perpetuate the myth that [significant numbers of] racial minorities will be attracted to Anglo congregations.
- Define the primary responsibility of congregations as supporting denominational initiatives, rather than defining the primary role of the denomination as providing resources to congregations.
- Consider the #1 source of creativity to be denominational agencies and not congregational leaders.
- Fail to realize that theological diversity and large numbers of worshippers are incompatible goals.[2]

Do these sound familiar? These counterproductive strategies are writ large in the Association's playbook. A few of these strategies (I'll let you decide which) have been elevated to the status of dogma, a word not frequently used in our tradition but which carries the mantle of immutable truth. This is our playbook today, one with which we are rushing headlong into the future.

My goal in bringing these issues to light is twofold: first, to encourage clergy and lay leaders to recognize that sticking to the old rules will lead to our eventual demise; and second, to state emphatically that local congregations can bring about new and different rules to create renewed health and vitality.

What might some new game rules be? I'd like to offer some strategies that are applicable to clergy, lay leaders, and people in the pews. Let us together write new playbooks that will revitalize congregational life and create churches of meaning and purpose.

I hope the power of the following strategies lies in their simplicity. I make no call for new committees, task forces, or commissions. No group needs an increased budget. No one has to get on an airplane and fly anywhere. For the most part, these strategies don't even cost anything. Here's my list:

1. Knowledge Is Power

An engaging body of literature about church life is within easy reach. Much of the literature is in the form of inexpensive, slim volumes that are easily read. Even the titles of these books are provocative: *Transforming Congregations for the Future; 44 Ways to Increase Church Attendance; What People Expect From Church; We've Never Done It Like This Before; Small Congregation, Big Potential; and The Passion Driven Church*, to name just a few.

These books provide extraordinary insight into the nature of congregational life. A bit of reading will bring fresh ideas and help clergy and lay leaders perceive their churches in previously unimagined ways, and will help them become more effective in their roles.

2. Visit Churches of Other Denominations

Visiting another congregation does not mean attending a neighborhood church for an interfaith or holiday service, when a church would attract outside visitors. Rather, pick a church of another faith where no one knows you, visit on a routine Sunday morning, and experience how it feels to be a newcomer. Some observers of congregational life suggest that first-time visitors will decide within eleven minutes whether to return a second time.

I visit churches of many faiths as part of my work, and eleven minutes is an interminable period of time in some of them. In the Christian context, a welcoming climate is referred to as the presence of God. What type of "presence" does your church communicate?

Visiting a church can be an unhappy experience. Many visitors feel they have stumbled onto a family reunion and perceive themselves as intruders. What is it like to be a visitor in your church? Are there friendly "grinners and greeters" near the entrance? Are visitors asked to sign the guest book? Do they receive name tags? Do active members of the church also wear nametags? Do ushers help visitors find a comfortable seat in the sanctuary? Do members accompany visitors to the coffee hour? Do visitors receive a follow-up note of welcome from the church later in the week?

Some churches form welcoming committees to greet visitors. Paradoxically, many of these churches see membership decline, as people in the pews believe that greeting visitors is not their job, but that of the welcoming committee. It is the task of all members to greet people they do not recognize. Even the most introverted person can say to a visitor, "We're glad you visited." By the way, does your church schedule visitors' Sundays, times when current members invite potential new members? A large percentage of church members of all faiths say they first came to church because someone they knew invited them. In my experience, inviting others to church is a practice we need to encourage.

We seem to be comfortable telling friends about good movies, books, and restaurants, but not about a good church. Many UUs also rarely, if ever, speak of their spiritual journeys or their faith. We need to overcome this reluctance. This is not strident evangelism, but rather sharing heartfelt examples of the meaning of the church in our lives. For more that twenty years I lived in New England and often heard, "The best religion is kept private." I also recall someone citing a statistic that UUs invited others to visit their churches about once every twenty-eight years!

3. The Truth Shall Set Us Free

UUs maintain they seek the truth from many sources. My experience is that we seek truth from a selected number of sources, those not in conflict with our current point of view. We are shockingly closed-minded to religious sources that are more conservative.

Believe it or not, liberal fundamentalism is alive and well in UU churches! The assumption is that if we do not subscribe to the theology of conservative faiths, there is nothing to be learned from them. For example, we conveniently overlook the fact that theologically conservative churches are vastly superior in creating multicultural congregations.

I often work with churches that hold conservative beliefs, and many of them are significantly ahead of UU churches in addressing issues of congregational life. These traditions are better at recruiting new members and keeping them involved for longer periods of time. They expect higher levels of commitment. They are more effective at stewardship. They also have the ability to "plant" new churches. A UU congregation intentionally starting a new church in the past fifty years is a rarity. Even the word "planting," familiar in many faiths, is foreign to us.

(It is important to note that newly formed or conservative churches are not the be-all and end-all of churches today. All churches have their strengths and weaknesses. For example, our movement has made great strides in areas such as gay and lesbian rights.)

Let's take a look at how one church was planted. Rick Warren is a Baptist minister who set out from Texas for Southern California in 1980 with his wife and two-year old daughter. Their worldly possessions were towed behind in a U-Haul trailer. They dreamed of planting a new church. Within fifteen years, the Saddleback Community Church they founded in Orange County had grown to 15,000 members and was sited on a seventy-four-acre campus. (During that fiteen-year period, the church moved seventy-nine times before finding a permanent home!)

Warren's book, *The Purpose Driven Church*, is compelling.[3] Warren's theology is not ours, but we cannot discount the skill, intelligence, and hard work required to accomplish such a feat. The twenty-year old Saddleback Church has twice as many members as all UU churches in California combined.

As of April 2004 Warren's most recent book, *The Purpose Driven Life*, has been on the *New York Times* best-seller list for sixty-four weeks, with over eight million copies sold.[4] The book's basic premise is, "Why am I here?" This volume of sales indicates that a lot of people, millions in fact, don't know why they are here on this earth. Should not our faith offer answers to people who have compelling questions about their purpose in life?

In the small town in Massachusetts where I live, a number of churches are struggling. An Episcopal church closed its doors, a Congregational church "nested" an ethnic Korean congregation in order to survive, and the local congregation of the American Baptist Church (the "liberal" wing of Baptists) has dwindled to a handful of people at Sunday worship. Meanwhile, the Mormons recently completed construction of a stunning $34 million temple at the edge of town, paid for in cash.

Seismic shifts in American religious life are underway. We do not comprehend the shifts that have occurred around us, nor how they affect the future of liberal religion. Conservative churches, surprisingly, may offer a perspective that can be of significant assistance to our liberal faith. Princeton University Professor Robert Wuthnow writes, "Liberalism [in religion] should not be a reaction to fundamentalism, but rather a counter-culture to secularism. It needs to present itself as a third way."[5]

This "third way," is the message of anti-secularism. UU churches should challenge members to lead lives that go against the prevailing consumer culture. It is here that conservative churches leap ahead of liberal faiths, in calling their members to become the kind of people God wants them to become. UU churches should draw people away from their day-to-day lives and bring them to a place and a state of mind that is tangibly and palpably different than they experience anywhere else.

4. Our Vision and Mission Statements Do Not Serve Us Well

It bears repeating that in many UU churches, mission or vision statements are built on concepts such as, "seeking truth." These statements are vague at best, and are not internalized by the minister or the congregation. Such statements do not touch the heart and soul, or challenge people to rise to the occasion. Our mission statements should communicate unambiguously that being a member of a UU congregation should change one's life in some fundamental way. One of my favorite mission statements comes from contemporary theologian Sarah Coakley, who attended a girl's school in England founded by a group of feminists in the 1860s. The mission statement of that school is, "To create women who can beat men at their own game." No ambiguity here!

5. Raise the Expectations of Membership

In many UU churches, newcomers attend a three-week orientation session, the third week of which is a potluck, and they're in! All too frequently, the attitude is one of reluctance to ask people to make a commitment to the church. We fear we will offend people if we ask them for too much.

People are more open to new ideas when they first join a church than at any other time. If the expectations of membership are undefined, churches will create lukewarm and half-hearted parishioners. People are drawn to churches because they wish to be a meaningful part of meaningful organizations. I suspect they leave not because we ask too much, but because we ask too little.

The Association has not been helpful in this regard. A book about membership titled *Belonging*, written by the Commission on Appraisal, contains this observation:

> The Commission has found a number of issues that trigger discussion, and, at times, confuse our understanding of the meaning of membership. These issues lead to provocative questions that can provide the basis for discussion and discernment. We do not propose answers to these questions.[6]

If the UUA's Commission on Appraisal cannot define what it means to be a member of a UU church, where does this deficiency leave us? Unitarian Universalism's hands-off attitude stems from a reluctance to ask people to make a commitment to the faith.

Lutheran minister Michael Foss has articulated one of the most succinct concepts of membership I have ever discovered. When people join the Prince of Peace Lutheran Church in Burnside, Minnesota, they are told, "You will be cared for here, but at some time you will be called upon to care for others."[7] This conveys that indeed, you may come here when in need; but at some point you will be asked to help someone else, in turn. This balances the equation in terms of the church serving people, but also calling people to serve.

A model of membership that I particularly favor is, "Three level ministry." First, people are encouraged to attend worship regularly. As noted, many UU churches do not expect regular worship attendance as part of active membership.

Second, parishioners can do something for themselves, such as sing in the choir, attend a book discussion group, join a men's or women's group, or take part in church programs. Third, members are expected to engage in a ministry to those in the congregation who may be in need, or an outreach effort beyond the congregation that serves others.

UU churches should claim their rightful *authority* and *responsibility* to set expectations and guidelines for membership. When joining a professional association, enrolling in a class at an educational institution, or becoming a member of any type of organization, we expect there will be rules and regulations. We follow them without question. This is the nature of organizations.

In UU churches, however, we allow members to set their own rules and level of involvement. Left without guidance, people often set the level far too low, by design or by default, or from a shortage of inspiring role models of how to be a member. This practice creates lukewarm and uncommitted members, and weakens the congregation as a whole.

6. Raise the Expectations of Charitable Giving

Giving 10 percent of one's income should become the norm in UU churches. Every UU congregation I have ever worked with has a few members who believe it is a privilege to tithe to the church. However, they may not do so if the opportunity is not set before them. Annual pledge drives in UU churches should offer parishioners the option to give 10 percent of their incomes, or more. Many financial planners claim that middle class Americans could double their charitable giving and not notice any difference in their standard of living. Believe it or not, just about every UU congregation could double the income from its annual pledge drive with ease. Shocking but true!

Generous parishioners and generous congregations go hand in hand. Most mainline and conservative churches have an outreach line item of at least 10 percent of their operating budgets. This is in addition to denominational and district dues. Thus, the institution of the church also gives 10 percent, a policy that is written into the by-laws.

A Methodist congregation near my home gives away 29 percent of its annual budget. But even this pales in comparison to the Memorial Drive Presbyterian Church in Houston that gives away a dollar for the needs of the world for every dollar it spends on itself. The people who sit in the pews of these churches are little different from UUs in terms of their socio-economic status. UU churches of all sizes and assets should allocate a minimum of 10 percent of their operating budgets to outreach.

In implementing this policy church leaders are likely to hear some people say, "I'll choose where I wish to give my money, and don't want the church making that decision for me." Leaders might properly respond to this comment with these words: "Thank you for your opinion, but the church is going to do this anyway." Do not let a small, vocal group distract the larger congregation from this goal. It is the right thing to do. Besides, chances are good that those who complain come from the ranks of the lowest-level donors. Generosity begets generosity, and conversely, miserliness begets miserliness.

7. Create a Climate for Effective Leadership

The Board of Trustees at the UU Church in Rochester, Minnesota hosts a dinner each quarter for new members. The officers provide an overview of how the church works, and newcomers get a glimpse into congregational life. The board chair then issues a very important invitation to these new members, which is: "During the time you are in this congregation, we encourage you to aspire to a position of leadership." This statement gives newcomers blanket permission to become church leaders. The by-laws of that congregation also call for one new member to serve on every committee of four people or more.

This policy of encouraging ever-renewing leadership contrasts sharply with many churches, where newcomers have to "pay their dues," or put in a certain number of years before being considered qualified for leadership roles.

William Easum is a Methodist minister who extols, "Permission-granting churches, those congregations that do not worship at the altar of control but allow parishioners the freedom and resources to create new ministries."[8] Vital and healthy congregations encourage parishioners to begin new outreach efforts when they encounter suffering in the world, even if these are ad hoc groups working on a short-term basis.

Churches that have a New Opportunities Seed Fund can create such initiatives. Having such a fund empowers any member to act when he or she encounters something in the world that is just not right. This approach is called the "equipping church," because rank and file members know the church will equip them to do the job effectively, will stand behind them, and will provide working capital if necessary. An excellent way to create a New Opportunities Seed Fund is to begin giving away the offering each Sunday, part of which can be put into this new fund.

The equipping church, with is emphasis on spontaneous initiatives, is more compatible with the highly scheduled lives of contemporary churchgoers, and considerably more appealing to many people than being asked to serve a three-year term on a standing committee. The small-group ministry approach taking root in UU congregations is an excellent example of the permission-granting concept, as long as these groups have a service component and are not merely discussion groups.

8. Fill the Most Visible Roles First

In many churches, leadership roles are filled according to the organizational chart. The board chair is selected first, followed by the vice-chair. The treasurer and members of the finance committee are next, followed by other board officers, then the board as a whole. This selection process often relegates people with exceptional talent to working around conference tables with only themselves as company, focused on the administration, finance, and maintenance of the church.

Key leaders should also serve in visible, "front line" aspects of ministry. These include mission and outreach, community programs, and the all-important welcoming and membership aspects of a friendly and engaging congregation. These are the key roles that should be filled first.

9. Sheep and Goats

While our principles call for the respect and dignity of every person, not all members serve the congregation well. Unfortunately, some people come to church with their own agendas, which may not benefit the congregation as a whole. In fact, the persistent efforts of six to ten people can turn a healthy congregation into a dysfunctional church.

When people come to church, they don't want to get into conflict with their friends and neighbors. This is not to say that disagreements will never occur. Churches are human institutions and good decisions are often the result of ideas from differing points of view. However, most parishioners will walk away from conflict when it arises in church, leaving those who created the conflict in a position of inordinate strength.

A friend of mine is a Presbyterian minister and he related an incident in his church regarding a group of perennially disgruntled members. He and the board chair gathered this group together and said to them, "We love you dearly, but we're going to ask you to take a leave of absence from the church for a year or two, to think and pray about whether this church is truly the one for you." As much as we desire our churches to serve all in our midst, some people should be cut loose—perhaps temporarily, perhaps permanently.

And Finally

In his book *Excellent Protestant Congregations*, Paul Wilkes writes about churches not bound by geography; churches that reach beyond their comfort zones; churches that are deliberate about taking their members to new levels; and churches that don't inform people about God, but help them experience God.[9]

These are churches that give people both something to reach for, and something to hold onto. This is the church I want to belong to.

Chapter Nine

A Visual Portrait of Your Church's Meaning and Values

As I arrived for a recent event at All Souls Unitarian Church in Tulsa, Oklahoma, a sizeable group of people stood before a large painting. The Senior Minister, Marlin Lavanhar, was animatedly describing the contents of this painting.

Lavanhar recounted that about a year before, he had visited the corporate office of a parishioner. A painting on display in the lobby depicted a number of seemingly unrelated objects that were placed in the artwork to represent the values, culture, and ideals of that company.

Lavanhar returned to the church and immediately commissioned a professional artist, a member of the church, to create a painting that represented All Souls Church. It was this painting that he was describing in such vivid terms.

Several church members commented on the painting while I was there, saying how helpful it was not only to members, but also to church shoppers and to un-churched people who came into the building for weddings, funerals, and other events. The painting gave all who passed by a visual conception of what the church and the faith were all about.

What's in the painting? I'll provide a glimpse of some of the objects but I don't want to reveal them all. Churches wanting to use this approach should use their imaginations to create their own paintings.

At the bottom of the painting is a colonial era table, representing the church's roots in that historical era. On the table rests a Bible, representing our Jewish and Christian heritage. Resting on the Bible is a book by Ralph Waldo Emerson, representing sources beyond Scripture that also hold meaning and inspiration. A third book is atop the other two, a bound volume with no title, representing the future of the church that has yet to be written.

The centerpiece of the painting is a large glass vase, filled with a glorious multitude of flowers. The flowers represent the members of the church and the vase represents the church in which they gather. The vase also contains water, a source of all life.

On the table lay a dead oak leaf, representing all who had been part of the congregation over time, but who were no longer present. Also on the table was . . . well, I'll let you decide what items should be in your church's painting.

CHAPTER TEN

Leadership Is the Key Ingredient

Who is the REAL leader? He stands face-to-face

with his circumstances and does not flinch. She confronts

the challenge head on. He is keenly aware of his strengths,

his resources, his options, his limits, his opportunities,

and the strengths of his team—for exactly what they are.

He uses all of his available skills and talents to create solutions

that minimize loss and maximize gain.

She faces difficult circumstances with muscular resolve.

> —from a flier for Reality Leadership Training Programs
> offered by The Injoy Group, Atlanta, Georgia

A T A CHURCH CONFERENCE I attended recently, a representative of the Injoy Group handed me the leadership flier quoted above. This young man could have been a model for the "dress for success" crowd. He wore a handsome navy suit, a crisp white shirt with gold collar pin and gold cuff links, an expensive silk tie, and highly polished wingtips. He projected a corporate image of self-assurance and confidence.

I was struck with how different The Injoy Group's leadership approach is from clergy and lay leaders who do not wear designer clothes and project an attitude of service rather than a hard-driving certitude.

The approach described by the Injoy Group reminded me of the "great man" theory of leadership described by Harvard Business School Professor Ronald Heifetz in his book, *Leadership Without Easy Answers*.[1] The "great man" theory (but not great women, it seems) of 200 years ago posits that men such as Napoleon Bonaparte or George Washington possessed indomitable traits of leadership that carried them (and us) to our destinies. If we can identify these traits and replicate them in others, we could create great men today.

A quote in the Injoy Group flier also stated, "The first responsibility of a leader is to define reality." In my experience, churches frequently defy reality in the way they are organized and managed. I am drawn to the church because of these inconsistencies and because religion is, "Full to overflowing with spectacular improbabilities" as author Karen Fields observed.[2] To me, church life is not prone to an exacting analysis, or to the "identify the problem and solve it" approach.

A Glimpse into Congregational Life

In my experience, the most significant leadership issues are twofold: an entrenched status quo, along with a lack of courage among clergy and lay leaders to confront established patterns of congregational life. Many congregations are anxious about the future, yet shackled to the past. Clergy and lay leaders are often more concerned about achieving consensus among parishioners than bringing a renewed health and vitality to their congregations.

What Are the Real Issues?

As a parish consultant I receive phone calls from potential church clients pertaining mainly to membership and financial concerns. Membership is on a plateau or in decline, and the annual pledge drive has not reached its dollar goal. These calls are often tinged with anxiety. Will I come and help?

I often use an iceberg analogy with churches and view member-ship and the annual pledge drive as the portions visible above the water line. Larger issues lie below the surface. Primary among these are clergy and lay leaders who view themselves not as leaders but as caretakers, who perceive their duty as keeping the church on a steady keel in still waters until others come along and replace them.

Two issues loom large in congregational leadership. First, clergy and lay leaders often exhibit a lack of understanding about the nature of the churches they serve. In most seminaries today, issues of "practi-cal ministry" are rarely included in the curriculum. (I once taught a course at a seminary and discovered that during the 1970s and 1980s students were told that leadership was a dirty word, and as ordained ministers they should have nothing to do with it!) In general, lay lead-ers are also unfamiliar with and often uninterested in the major writ-ers about church life; or the wealth of books, articles, and church-related resources that are readily available to them.

I once gave a brief talk on this subject titled, "A Curious Phenome-non," and pointed out a natural human curiosity about things that touch our lives. We may be interested in antiques, backyard birds, phi-losophy, baseball, archeology, or how to fix a leaky faucet, for exam-ple. It seems natural that we would go to the library, the bookstore, or search on-line to find information about our interests.

This curiosity seems to stop when it comes to church. Many con-gregational leaders do not realize that information about the nature, character, and behavior of churches even exists. Moreover, they are of-ten reluctant to utilize these resources even when provided. Many de-cisions in churches are made by well-educated, highly capable, well-intentioned people who would never in their professional lives make decisions based on little more than intuition.

The second issue of congregational leadership that I encounter re-lates to Lyle Schaller's observation that, "Many church leaders feel their job is not to expand ministry, but to minimize expenses." [3] This attitude is most prevalent in congregations that use the operating budget as the centerpiece of the annual pledge drive, and there is an acute sense (or considerable anxiety) about how much things cost at church. When the budget is presented, usually at the annual meeting, the reaction among congregants can be, "Why do we have to pay so much for. . . ." An endless number of items can appear on this list, sometimes beginning with the minister's salary.

While membership and stewardship are the reasons that lead most congregations to request my assistance, about 90 percent of my work is below the water line of that iceberg. These include issues such as a congregation's unique history and tradition; its role in the community; what the congregation believes it is called to do in this place and time; how it welcomes visitors on Sunday morning; how the church integrates new members into the life of the congregation; how a church develops a climate of encouraging people to aspire to leadership roles; how all the parts of church life require effective leadership, and how being involved in the church can be a meaningful spiritual experience.

Once I have reviewed these issues with a congregation's leadership and gained a clearer understanding of a congregation's unique identity, we then move on to membership and stewardship. This sequence allows me to take the perspective that stewardship begins when a first-time visitor arrives at church, becomes a member, and extends throughout the life of the congregation, including estate planning and bequest options. Stewardship is an essential ministry of the church, an integral part of congregational life and not an "add on" when the annual pledge drive is conducted. *It is not possible to have ineffective leadership and disengaged members for eleven months of the year, then expect the annual pledge drive to be wildly successful in the twelfth.* Yet all too frequently, that is what I, as a parish consultant, am asked to make happen.

Leadership is the key ingredient in raising money successfully, or in any other endeavor in the church. Unfortunately, the prevailing view is that leadership orientation, training, and continuing education are required in the secular world, but are optional or even unnecessary at church.

Congregations perform a disservice in electing or appointing capable men and women to leadership positions, then expecting them magically to manage their roles effectively. This is just not fair, as newly appointed leaders frequently inherit an abundance of institutionalized bad habits of which they were unaware when they accepted the job. In my experience, most bad habits and problems in UU churches stem from low expectations of membership, low expectations of charitable giving, and attempts to keep members satisfied. This combination of factors creates systemic weaknesses in churches of all sizes.

More Complex than Meets the Eye

Sometimes congregational life looks so easy. When people gather at church they wish to be kind to one another and experience the presence of the sacred. Parishioners expect a higher order of relationships. They wish to set aside petty differences and squabbles, and work toward a greater good. As a result, when difficulties arise in the human institution of the church, parishioners may become reactionary, as their distress can be more disconcerting than it would be in a secular setting. Thus, effective leadership is a more complex and sensitive issue than it appears to be; one that requires good judgment, an open mind, and the knowledge of why people behave in certain ways at church.

Are Leaders Born or Made?

In my work with churches I find two general types of leaders. The first is the more visible, people who naturally assume leadership roles in their personal and professional lives. Perhaps these are the so-called born leaders. They serve on church boards and willingly seek roles of influence and authority.

The other type of leader is the behind-the-scenes personality, ever-diligent people who quietly ensure the maintenance and operation of the church. These generous souls coordinate potluck dinners, arrange for flowers, oversee the work of the plumber or the electrician, and often write checks when extra money is needed. These church pillars may not view themselves as leaders at all. They just love the church and want to make sure things are done well.

I don't believe leadership is a "born vs. made" polarity. The two leadership types just noted, along with a variety as infinite as the number of human personalities in a given church, are essential for the well being of a religious community. The more important question is, "Does the church create a climate in which all types of leadership thrive?"

In more conservative faiths an additional issue is considered: whether a particular role will aid in the person's spiritual growth. If not, the candidate is not selected. These churches constantly seek "the next spiritual level" for their congregants.

Traits of Effective Leadership

I conclude with a few traits that I find essential in effective church leaders. First, I expect a leader to be knowledgeable about the subject at hand—to have done some homework. A leader's level of knowledge should be above rank and file members.

With parish ministers I permit considerable allowances. Parish ministry is infinitely more complex today than in decades past, and sometimes a minister's lot is not a happy one. Ministers are expected to conduct worship effectively, preach eloquently, tell engaging children's stories, possess a prayerful bedside manner for visiting the sick, raise a prophetic voice, motivate volunteers, set an example for others, remain ever on call, oversee the administration and management of the church, practice at least one spiritual discipline, engage in interfaith work and denominational projects, and publish their writings—all with style, grace, and charm, seven days a week. The expectations are vast.

For me, the true test is whether the minister displays a genuine love for the church and its people. Parishioners instinctively know if a minister likes being around them. If this quality is present, church members are more likely to take on leadership roles and assume responsibilities that compliment the minister's strengths and weaknesses.

In addition, a critical element in leadership is the concept of "follower-ship." In sports, this is called, "being a team player." Leaders cannot lead people who do not recognize their authority to do so. UU churches should not be about the doctrine of the autonomous individual, but rather about the hard work of forming a people. Each of us needs to realize that our ideas may not always be the ones that hold sway. The more important issue is to create congregations that embody a higher calling and function effectively as a whole.

Clergy and lay leaders should call parishioners to rise to the occasion when the situation warrants. And congregants should respond. Church literature today contains many compelling stories about congregations challenged to carry out tasks they thought were beyond their abilities. This is a hallmark of an engaging church.

And Finally, Spirituality

Many thriving churches today base their success on adult spiritual development. When this ingredient is present, all things become possible. In my experience with mainline and liberal faiths, this element of religious life is absent.

On frequent occasions people have said to me, "We've been members of this church for six, [or eight, or ten] years and don't believe we are any more spiritual or religious people now than when we joined." These comments often contain a tinge of sadness and regret.

The prevailing culture in too many UU congregations is that churches offer programs that people attend. Parishioners are educated, informed, enlightened, fed, and entertained—but not challenged to lead lives of meaning and purpose.

My own spirituality is influenced by my upbringing in the "right or wrong" era of the Roman Catholic Church. I memorized my Catechism faithfully. The Ten Commandments were always on display, along with the crucifix and the portrait of Jesus. My world was one in which both priests and nuns wore only clerical garb and lived mysteriously behind closed doors in rectories and convents. They were afforded great respect.

As a youth I strived to be a good person under the guidance of the Catholic church, and still do today, though in a different theological context. But like those shaped by the civic faith of the 1950s, I remain uncertain about the direction of my own spiritual development. I seek religious guidance and leadership, and look to clergy to provide it.

To this day I have an automatic respect for ordained clergy. However, as a condition of my "followership" and my willingness to take on leadership roles in church, I expect clergy to set an example of how to lead a religious life. Some of my colleagues claim this is an unfair and unrealistic expectation of clergy, as they are mere mortals. But I know many exemplary lay people who abide by the church's ethical and moral standards. Clergy have no less an obligation.

It may be that a few "bad apples" have created a climate of distrust regarding clergy where one of respect used to prevail. Clergy must therefore be ever more vigilant in their personal and professional lives, to help restore a sense of the sacred in the congregation.

The spiritual trait I look for in a religious leader is trustworthiness, and how that is built and maintained. My experience is that congregants will be considerably more gracious and infinitely more forgiving in matters of congregational life if they trust and respect the leadership. In many churches this trust is in short supply, and a culture of control is more evident. Just about anything anyone wants to do requires approval from others, sometimes many others.

Much work needs to be done in this vineyard. Effective and courageous leadership is a rare commodity, one our churches should create and nurture at every opportunity. UU churches need leaders of vision and courage who do not function from an attitude of control, but who will help congregants discover the spark of the divine within themselves, and help people lead lives of meaning and purpose both in and outside the church.

CHAPTER ELEVEN

Why Stewardship Is a Constant Struggle

A FRIEND OF MINE REFERS to the annual pledge drive in his church as a "congregational root canal." For many churches, stewardship is a perennially vexing issue. Serving on the stewardship committee is often viewed as the most thankless task a church has to offer.

My intention in this chapter is to provide some hopeful words for those brave souls, clergy and lay, who are responsible for stewardship in their congregations. Stewardship should be a long-term ministry, not a disagreeable chore.

Effective stewardship needs to begin with some "end runs" around the conventional wisdom. Two examples come readily to mind. The first is that if the church sets a mission or vision, people will give. The second is the enduring but erroneous belief that better-written pledge letters, stewardship brochures, inspiring sermons, and heart-rending appeals from the pulpit will motivate parishioners to give more than they currently do.

The conventional wisdom does apply to the most generous parishioners, those who love the church and will give no matter what the stewardship message. Unfortunately, these are a minority of donors and in many instances are the most elderly. As time passes, these older members will become fewer and fewer, and the conventional wisdom will become less and less applicable.

More Difficult than It Appears

Each year we ask people to support the church, and we hope they do the right thing. For the generous souls just mentioned who have supported the church from time immemorial, this is an unchanging message and a heartfelt way of life. They believe in the church and are steadfast in their view that charitable giving is integral to a meaningful life and a strong faith.

Unfortunately, stewardship among 50–75 percent of the congregation as a whole is likely to reflect a pattern of low-level and same-level giving. People develop entrenched habits in the ways they spend money, for better or worse; including how much they give, if they give at all. These habits die hard. Sizeable numbers of church members may have no intention of increasing their charitable giving, no matter how much money they have, no matter what the church says, or what the mission might be. The stewardship message, however articulate, will go unheeded by 50–75 percent of the members in most UU congregations.

Parishioners (of many faiths) may also feel strongly that the church should have no influence whatsoever over what they decide to give. Robert Wuthnow discovered this attitude among respondents in surveys he has conducted. People believe their work, their money, and the church are completely separate elements in their lives. They do not grant the church any authority in their charitable decisions.[1]

Robert Wood Lynn, a former Lilly Endowment executive, has explored the issue of authority in his historical perspective of the language of religious philanthropy. The matter of "by what authority" the church asks for money has been debated for centuries. In times gone by, churches claimed a stronger moral authority over the lives of parishioners than is the case today.

Where Does Stewardship Begin?

Church literature often suggests that stewardship begins once people are in church, or when they learn of its mission. This view is shortsighted. Many stewardship decisions are made, by design or by default, long before parishioners set foot in the building.

The influence of the consumer culture on parishioners' lives cannot be overstated. For example, older people often shake their heads in disbelief at the amount of debt that younger generations routinely take on. Unfortunately, we live in a society that increasingly communicates, "No matter how much you have, you deserve more."

Arthur Simon, a Lutheran Minister and founder of the organization Bread for the World, writes in his book *How Much is Enough? Hungering for God in an Affluent Culture*: "The problem is not that we've tried faith and found it wanting, but that we've tried mammon and found it addictive. As a result, following the precepts of the church is inconvenient."[2]

On numerous occasions I've heard ministers in their seventies and eighties tell me about the advice they received from their elders. The old rule was: Of your income, give 10 percent to the church, save 10 percent, and live on the remaining 80 percent. The new rule seems to be: Live on 110 percent of your income, save nothing, and hope your investments and home equity increase in value.

Many parishioners may be over-extended financially, carry debt on more than one credit card, have high mortgage payments, and monthly payments for automobiles or other consumer goods. If so, churches will not engage these parishioners in meaningful stewardship conversations. An antidote to consumer spending is the increasing number of churches that offer financial planning courses based on religious principles. I heartily encourage this type of program for UU congregations. Programs are geared for people of all income levels, and include issues such as pension planning, proper amounts of insurance, strategies for paying college tuition, estate planning, and the appropriate use of credit.

The goal of these courses is not to maximize wealth, though this may be a pleasant by-product. Rather, the purpose is to help people of all faiths use the resources at their command to lead lives of meaning and purpose. This message, a bedrock principle in many Christian churches is: It is not just the 10 percent you give to the church that's important, but also what you do with the remaining 90 percent to help further the Kingdom on earth. Not our theology perhaps, but a compelling alternative to the incessant advertisements bombarding us to purchase ever more consumer goods, and to feel inferior if we cannot.

Where Does This Leave Us?

Clergy and lay leaders seeking advice about stewardship often look for some type of stewardship conference. Unfortunately, stewardship workshops and seminars do not serve congregations well. These events can best be described as the "teacher and student" approach. People who may or may not be knowledgeable about the subject lead stewardship seminars that range in length from a few hours to a day or a weekend course. Clergy and lay leaders attend these seminars hoping to learn fund-raising techniques that will work in their congregations.

Sometimes a church may see a short-term increase in giving as the result of a stewardship seminar. However, old patterns of giving tend to return very quickly. This happens because seminars do not take into account the unique and long-established culture of giving in each congregation, or the attitudes of parishioners toward the use of money in their lives. An Episcopal Bishop recently told me, "We've been having stewardship conferences in this diocese for ten years and I don't think they have made much difference at all."

John and Sylvia Ronsvalle have studied the charitable giving patterns or churchgoers for decades. Their studies indicate that charitable giving per member has increased since 1968, but this increase in giving lags behind larger increases in income. Charitable giving has declined as a percentage of what we have. The more we gain, the less we give.[3]

Unfortunately, even bedrock principles may be waning in influence. According to Catholic University Professor Dean Hoge and his colleagues:

Younger generations cannot be expected to respond to appeals for giving based on strong faith, or the teachings of the Old and New Testaments [the traditional Christian approach.] They are little different from secular people in how they think about monetary gifts."[4]

Each Church Has Its Own Charitable Identity

Effective stewardship strategies for congregations will not be devised in sixty-minute sessions at stewardship conference. The future of effective stewardship lies in the maxim that no two churches are alike.

Long-term, effective stewardship begins with an assessment of the giving culture of individual congregations. I call this a congregation's "charitable identity." (The way a congregation addresses financial matters as a whole can be considered its "financial identity.") If we do not understand parishioners' attitudes toward money in their lives, and these attitudes can vary dramatically from church to church, we will not create a language of stewardship that is resonant with them.

Once a congregation's charitable identity is determined, a tailor-made stewardship plan can then be crafted. Tailor-made stewardship plans are effective because they take into account a congregation's history and tradition, its geographic location, and local economic circumstances. Tailor-made plans also allow for financial issues that affect young, middle-aged, and older generations differently. These plans can also incorporate enlightened perspectives from many faiths, including some examples from non-Christian traditions. With a little help, clergy and lay leaders can learn to write tailor-made plans themselves. The next chapter provides some clues.

CHAPTER TWELVE

Money in the Church: A Guide for Clergy, Lay Leaders, and People in the Pews

THE SUBJECT OF MONEY is not just for those who are well to do or have plenty to give. Nor is money a subject only for the financially astute, those persons blessed with the gift of numbers or a background in finance or accounting. Money is an issue that affects congregants every day, in one form or another, for better or worse.

In this chapter we'll take a particular look at smaller churches, as about three-quarters of UU churches average fewer than 100 people at Sunday worship. I hasten to add that many issues regarding money in the small church relate to larger churches, as well. So this chapter is for everyone.

Before launching into the subject of money, let's explore the nature of the small church briefly, and by association, how certain issues apply to churches of all sizes. This will help us figure out how money is raised, how it flows in and out of the church, how much is saved for "rainy days" (if any), and who has control over it. Later in this chapter we'll explore the subject of tailor-made stewardship plans.

Members of small churches in many denominations often describe their communities in negative terms. These include, "We're not a large church," or, "We don't have an endowment," or, "We're not like the tall steeple church down the street." I prefer speaking of small churches in positive terms. After all, more small churches are in operation in this country than churches of any other size (in all denominations) and many of them are vital religious communities.

Besides, "small" is a relative term. In the world of independent, non-denominational churches, a large church is one that has at least 2,500 members. Using this definition, no UU church anywhere is big enough be a large church. So, a "large" church is in the eye of the beholder, and even large UU churches (550 members or more, according to Association guidelines) are aware of considerably larger churches of other denominations in the community, and may feel small in comparison.

The Times in Which We Live

These are not the best of times for churches of any size. Observers of the church world suggest that 85–90 percent of congregations in the United States are on a plateau in membership, or in decline. Thousands of churches have already closed, and gracious old buildings have been turned into condominiums, restaurants, and movie theatres.

Yet other churches with small or moderate-sized memberships and an apparent shortage of money remain active and vital. How can this be? Those in the Christian community regard the tenacity of churches as demonstrating the presence of God. A sense of divine intervention allows churches to remain afloat against seemingly insurmountable odds.

According to Scale

Episcopal minister Arlin Rothauge has written an extremely insightful book titled, *Sizing Up a Congregation*. He describes churches on the basis of number of people attending Sunday worship, not total membership. He uses the term "Family Church" to denote congregations that average fifty to seventy-five people or fewer on Sunday morning. [1]

Family-sized churches can be sited in rural areas, urban areas, and small towns. Some remain in huge old buildings whose sanctuaries were once filled with hundreds of members. Small churches are characterized by, "The rich rewards of familial support and profound sense of belonging," according to Rothauge. Newcomers, however, can perceive such a congregation as a family that is closed to them. This perception is often surprising to established members who believe their church is exceptionally friendly. (Mid-sized and large UU churches often display a "closed" attitude toward outsiders, as well.)

Newcomers who join a small congregation may sense they have been adopted rather than introduced as members. Newcomers to small churches often receive a kind of blessing from established members to become truly part of the community. Larger churches have one particular advantage over small churches, that being multiple points of entry and higher levels of anonymity (everyone does not already know everyone else), which can make it easier for newcomers to find their place in congregational life.

All too often, unfortunately, newcomers in churches of all sizes are perceived as "replacements." Church members hope newcomers will be "PLU," People Like Us, young people who act like old people, who will follow behind established members and eventually fill their roles when they no longer wish to carry on. New members are not expected to have new ideas; and in fact, old-timers may be resentful of recent arrivals who indeed bring new ideas. This attitude can be found in churches of all sizes. The way we "do church" is set, and new ideas are can be perceived as a challenge to the existing order.

What Does All This Have to Do with Money?

If a church of any size is unable to welcome newcomers graciously, the opportunity to discuss charitable giving is forever lost. Thus, genuine hospitality is the hallmark of an engaging congregation, both in terms of its ongoing life and its ability to maintain a healthy financial position. If people who visit on Sunday morning (usually the only route open in a small church) do not feel warmly welcomed, they will not return. Turning too many visitors into one-timers can jeopardize the long-term viability of a church. (Many newly formed churches actually engage staff people or volunteers in a Ministry of Hospitality.)

I frequently recommend that churches place the time of greeting as early in the Sunday Service as possible. This practice helps newcomers feel welcomed more quickly, alleviating the feeling of being lonely among strangers. I also recommend that people greet someone they don't know, if only to say a simple, "Hello." This takes a longer period of time than a brief greeting to those seated near you, but is time well spent. (I recall attending worship at an African Methodist Episcopal church, and the time of greeting took about twenty-five minutes. I shook hands with about 300 people that morning and felt truly welcomed.) I have a particular fondness for ministers who roam the aisles during the time of greeting, but realize this is not everyone's cup of tea.

I'm a frequent visitor to churches of many faiths, and the true hospitality of a congregation reveals itself during the coffee hour. In recent months I visited eight churches, and in every instance, after being greeted with "good morning" and handed an order of service at the door, not a single person spoke to me, even during the coffee hour. Numerous people I know who have gone church shopping tell me they avoid coffee hour like the plague.

I have some terrific stories about how I've been "greeted" at UU churches. Upon entering one church I saw a table with a "visitors" sign on it. I went that direction and noticed three people seated behind this table. Two were engaged in animated conversation with each other; and the third, a sorrowful looking person, was seated next to them. I approached this third person, who looked at me blankly and remained silent. So, I said, "I'm a visitor this morning. Do I do anything here?" In a loud, barking voice, she replied in a challenging way: "Well, are you coming only today, or are you coming back?" I suspect she had received no training or even any helpful suggestions about how to fulfill this important role.

Another favorite memory of being a visitor is standing in line for coffee at a large UU church, one that had two "pourers" filling people's coffee cups. A stack of assorted mugs stood beside the coffee pots. When I eventually made my way to the front of the line (progress was slow because parishioners engaged the pourers in lively conversation) the pourer I approached abruptly lost her cheerful demeanor, did not speak to me, and gave me a look that conveyed, "What do you want?" I told her I was a visitor and would like a cup of coffee. She selected a mug from the stack, filled it half full, and while handing it to me said somewhat mournfully, "It appears I've given you our least attractive mug."

I've also been the only person seated in the pew when I've visited churches. At one church, a middle-aged couple did join me in the pew, but after a minute or two moved ahead two pews, for no particular reason. I also recall visiting a church that had hymnals in small racks in the pews. Moments before the service began, the person in the next pew turned around and took the hymnal out of the rack in front of me.

I've also stood alone during coffee hours with the customary red cup that visitors are asked to use to identify themselves, and I've wandered around many a coffee hour by myself wearing my "guest" name tag. If readers would like to experience being an invisible person, try visiting a church. Many congregants do not know how to react when a stranger arrives at the door. People are indeed friendly, but usually to those they already know. Their lack of hospitality to newcomers is actually quite rude. When I relate incidents like this to others, their response is invariably, "Oh, something very much like that happened to me, too."

David Blanchard, minister of the First UU Society in Syracuse, New York, once wrote in his newsletter column that when visitors arrive at the church, some of them may believe that showing up is a public admission that their lives have not been made whole, and they feel vulnerable. Everyone in the pews needs to be cognizant of the fact that visiting the church we find so welcoming can be an unnerving experience for a newcomer.

Beyond Greetings

It bears repeating that the most critical issue in the long-term health of any church is what membership means. This includes a commitment of time, effort, and money in some measure. Clergy and lay leaders are often hesitant to ask people to do too much or to give very much, fearing that people will be turned off. This distant attitude might have worked well with older generations who believed in the institution of the church from day one, but it generally does not with people born after 1965.

Church literature suggests that people born after 1965 are theologically more conservative than liberal, and are seeking meaningful spiritual journeys. They are seeking a faith that expects a commitment of them. They do not expect this journey to be easy. Churches that are vague about the meaning of membership, or that have low-expectation policies established many years ago that are now ingrained in the culture will most likely see these potential new members pass them by.

Over the past twenty years, as a general rule, churches that grew in membership and in financial strength were those that set higher expectations.

Finally, We Get to Money

Some churches struggle financially, wondering where the next dollar is coming from. Others have large endowments and more money than they know what to do with. Some churches fund generous outreach programs joyfully, while other churches hang onto every nickel for dear life. Thus, clergy, lay leaders, and people in the pews may perceive the use of money in the church in dramatically different ways.

Some churches are in affluent areas while others are in poor neighborhoods. It is entirely possible that churches with drastically different financial circumstances might be located in adjacent communities. As a result, there is no single stewardship formula or method of church finance that applies to churches as a whole.

In fact, no two churches, even of the same denomination, are similar in their history and tradition, and no two are alike in how they handle money. While some similarities exist, each church has its own way of addressing financial issues, depending on habit, custom, and personalities involved.

However, it is important to recall that Lyle Schaller's line of demarcation is whether churches and their leaders function from an attitude of scarcity or an attitude of abundance, as each becomes a self-fulfilling prophecy.

My belief is that churches need to determine their own "charitable identities." Engaging the congregation to answer the following questions can help accomplish this:

- What is the current attitude, or "mindset" toward money in the church? In too many instances, the prevailing attitude is one of scarcity and secrecy. Churches need to create a climate in which charitable giving is the hallmark of a life well lived. Being a generous person or family is one of life's great privileges. Creating this attitude is primary—the church's operating budget is secondary. This attitude must begin with the leadership and filter down.

- Who controls the money? If the same people have made financial decisions for years or perhaps decades on end, a conservative approach to financial issues will prevail. The great UU paradox is that we claim to be liberal theologically, but behave as though we are archconservative financially.

- How is money spent? If most of the time, effort, and money go into institutional maintenance, the church will have difficulty attracting and keeping new members because they may not be willing to pay financial obligations that were incurred by others. If parishioners are asked to fund the operating budget instead of being called to become generous people, their giving is likely to remain limited. Vital congregations give away a larger than average share to outreach. These churches, surprisingly, often reflect little anxiety about money.

☙ What should people be asked to give? Giving 10 percent of income, or making a plan to reach 10 percent within a three-year period should be the expectation in UU churches, regardless of size. Congregations should ask parishioners to give a percentage of their income, not an amount such as the average pledge of the congregation as a whole.

Don't Be Afraid to Ask!

Recognize that people view money differently. Some people may be overextended financially. Others may have been raised in non-religious households and have no concept of stewardship. Others may have fallen into low-level giving habits for reasons they cannot articulate. Yet others may simply be miserly, not sharing with the church or anyone else. A sizeable group may be pursuing the good life with abandon, purchasing all that money can buy. Thus, the traditional "Theme of the year" stewardship message is one-dimensional and will reach only a small segment of the congregation at best.

The stewardship message should be to share in adequate measure, so that we may go about our day-to-day lives in good conscience, and be able to sleep at night. Aren't we privileged to be part of a community of faith that can create a better world?

In regard to small churches, keep in mind that traditional stewardship approaches, with their "give more to do more" appeals, may not applicable. Being a member of a small church can be tiring in that people already wear many hats. Giving more to do more may not be an appealing option. This factor does not mean that members of small churches are permitted to give less. It means that small churches can increase their outreach giving. The healthiest of small churches have a clear "vocation," something they do well, toward which they focus their time, energy, and money.

Finally, despite all this talk about church finance, money is actually a secondary issue. Churches of all sizes that create a vibrant life, a tangible presence of the sacred, and a habit of reaching out to serve will not worry about money. Stewardship is not about asking people for money. Stewardship concerns what kind of people the church calls us to become, and how a community of faith uses the resources at its command to serve with love and compassion. It is about LUKE 12: 48, "To whom much has been given, much is expected." From congregations with endowments, even more will be demanded.

The people who sit in the pews in small churches, and indeed all churches, are called to give, not to hoard. Surely this is the bedrock principle on which our churches must be built.

CHAPTER THIRTEEN

Why the UUA's New Congregations Initiative Will Fail

I N MAY OF 2003 the UUA's New Congregation Formation Task Force made a series of bold recommendations. The most notable is the formation of fifty new large, multi-staff churches over the next five years, each with 1,500–3,000 members.

A second bold recommendation is to invest from $800,000 to $1.2 million in each of these new congregations, a total of $40 million to $50 million.[1]

I suspect that Task Force members were well intentioned and well meaning. However, it is highly unlikely that even one church of this size will ever be founded. Let's examine the multitude of reasons why.

A Past We Cannot Ignore

We begin with recent history. The 1992 UUA Directory lists 1,029 congregations. In the spring 2004, the Association reports 1,008. (This figure does not include thirty-five congregations in Canada that no longer belong to the Association.) After accounting for the separation of Canadian congregations, a net gain of four churches in twelve years is not heartening. Based on anecdotal data, this gain of four churches is the result of about 135 new congregations being formed (mostly small fellowships) while 131 existing churches closed.

These figures raise two issues about growth of the number of churches in the Association. First, net growth in UU churches in the past ten years has been about one congregation of forty to fifty members per year. Is it realistic to believe that fifty new congregations, each thirty to sixty times larger in size, will spring up in half that time?

Given that UU churches attracted so few people in the past decade and are currently losing younger people, why would tens of thousands of people suddenly come streaming in through the doors? In fact, fifty new churches of 3,000 members each would double the current membership of 150,000 adults within five years. Is this notion truly plausible?

The second issue is that most new churches begun since 1990 range in membership from less than a dozen to 145. Only a few have more than 150 members and none report over 200. Most are in suburban or rural areas (Homer, Alaska; Poway, California; Ellijay, Georgia). The New Congregations Task Force report recommends that fifty new churches be started in metropolitan areas, and that a great deal of "specialized training" will be provided.

How does the Association plan to provide specialized training for the metropolitan strategy when no one has had any experience in starting large churches in metropolitan areas for fifty years? This specialized training will not come from attending seminars led by Christian-oriented organizations such as the Alban Institute that serves churches differing dramatically from UU congregations in their nature, character, and theology.

Planting Churches

The last time our religious movement saw new churches planted in a metropolitan area was the result of A. Powell Davies' extraordinary work in the 1940s and 50s. Davies was the most prolific church planter since the days of circuit-riding men and women in the 1800s. But even he managed less than one new church per year over twenty years, and that was during an era when church attendance was the highest in American history. Today, the churches he founded range in membership from 225 to 895. None ever reached 1,500 members, let alone 3,000.

Regarding the metropolitan strategy, the largest concentration of UU churches, UUs themselves, UU leadership, and indeed the Association's headquarters are in the state of Massachusetts. Since 1990 only one new fellowship has been founded in the entire state. This lone "Meeting" as it calls itself, has sixty-one members, meets in a Methodist church, and is located in the town of Great Barrington, near the New York/Connecticut state line, as far distant from Boston as geographically possible. It is also important to note that this church was started by a group of hearty souls on their own, without any denominational extension funds or support.

If the most significant concentration of UU resources in the country has not founded a single new congregation in its own backyard in the past decade or more, how will fifty new churches, each with thousands of members, be founded in five years? And from what source will the $40 million to $50 million come to accomplish this feat?

Numerous Issues to Ponder

The New Congregation Formation Task Force also overlooked a number of other fundamental ingredients for starting a large church. In most instances a charismatic leader is necessary to found a large church—someone with a commitment to ministry and a "fire in the belly" for evangelism. I would not characterize this as the prevailing UU culture.

While we claim to heed prophetic voices, we are similar to mainline Protestant denominations that exhibit mistrust of strong leadership. Our behavior reflects a deeply entrenched bias that decisions made by groups and committees, or via the democratic process, are safer than those made by individuals.

Unfortunately, the Task Force is using a traditional, small church model, i.e., committees, boards, strategic plans, and recommending that everything be made bigger. This is not the way a large church is founded or operates.

For example, in most large-scale churches, congregational deci-sion-making does not exist. Rather, leadership emanates from the minister and a small group of core leaders. In my experience, church boards and lay leaders in UU congregations of any size would not per-mit ministers to exercise the power and authority that ministers in large churches routinely exert. Power and authority from the top is the key to the success of a large church, as this minimizes internal dissent and binds people to a strongly articulated goal.

Newly formed churches today are most often planted by men (rarely women) who perceive a powerful call to ministry. This ap-proach is somewhat a throwback to the times when people like Martin Luther King (Senior) felt called to preach and just started a church. More often than not, these venturesome preachers of an-other era had little seminary training, if any, and their churches might be characterized as "storefront."

Large Churches Sometimes Grow
from Small Seeds

Many of today's large churches began as "house churches," led by people who experienced an unmistakable call to ministry. On occa-sion, these fledgling congregations grew to 10,000 members or more. These churches, predominantly Christian, are based on the premise that if God intends a church to grow, it will. If not, it won't.

The power of the message is the primary ingredient, the cornerstone of the large church, not staff and buildings. In my experience, most UUs don't believe we have a powerful, life-changing message, the bedrock principle on which large churches are built.

From Large to Large

Another method of starting a large church involves people referred to as "church planters," people who currently belong to a large congregation.

A new large-church start centers around a minister identified as having a strong vision, enthusiasm, energy, training, experience in a large church setting, a knack for effective evangelism, a track record in leading an exemplary life, and a conversion experience that has changed his life and is retold as a source of religious authority.

Accompanying this minister are lay leaders who have considerable experience in the large church environment as well, are viewed as living faithful lives, are highly trusted, and are specially trained in the art of founding a large church. These lay people are also likely to tithe.

Using this method, a large church will "release" 1,000 members, along with the specially trained minister, to plant a new church. This approach ensures almost automatic success, as a sizeable congregation, skilled staff, highly committed lay people, and adequate resources are part of a new church from the start. Such a church may rent a high school auditorium, send out a community-wide mailing, and on the first Sunday of worship draw a crowd of 1,500 or more.

A mega-church in Illinois planted three new large churches in a single year, by releasing thousands of current members. These new churches were of different denominations! One was Baptist, one was Church of the Brethren, and the third was nondenominational. This approach is simply not part of UU thinking or practice, nor is it feasible since no UU church has a membership large enough to permit sending out so many members to establish a new congregation.

The Prime Ingredient

The New Congregation Task Force also did not take into account the primary requisite in the success of large churches—a set of core beliefs. These core beliefs are usually the divinity of Jesus Christ and a reliance on Scripture. A non-negotiable set of beliefs is the element that permits a large and diverse membership to transcend its differences, and holds members together in a community of faith. This core set of beliefs explains why conservative churches are more effective in achieving a level of racial diversity that moderate and liberal faiths have been unable to accomplish.

Right offhand I don't see Unitarian Universalism moving toward a central theology to which all would subscribe.

Talkin' 'bout My Generation

The Task Force also failed to recognize that younger generations (in general) are not more liberal than previous generations, but are more conservative, both politically and theologically. Many are seeking a community of faith that will help them achieve a meaningful spiritual life.

With the UU insistence on freedom of the individual, "commitment to the church" and "leading meaningful spiritual lives" are not phrases often heard in UU churches. Unitarian Universalism is out of step with the times. We try to "push our product" (how can we get more people into our programs) rather than figuring out who newcomers to our congregations might be, what they seek in a community of faith, and how our churches can communicate with and engage them. We do not know who the new members of tomorrow will be, or what attracts them to church. These are primary elements in the founding of large churches.

Noticeably absent in the Task Force's recommendations is evangelism, a word and a practice that most UUs are uncomfortable with, and that many abhor. In most UU churches, the long-standing belief is, "If people are lucky, they will find us." This is not a formula to grow a large church.

An Ever-elusive Diversity

Author Lyle Schaller has also pointed out, "Churches that proclaim 'our strength is our diversity' will see the vast majority of first-time visitors pass them by, seeking a church with greater clarity."[2] Yet the plan for new UU churches is for them to be multi-racial and diverse theologically. Unless something radical emerges, the only way we will achieve racial diversity is for UUs to travel from their home churches and attend worship in ethnic congregations.

Why haven't we achieved diversity since we so eagerly seek racial minorities? Church literature today is replete with references to racial minorities preferring ethnic churches rather than attempting to blend into Anglo congregations. Alas, UUs are grossly uninformed about religious practice in the United States, and stand nobly against the tide of what people seek in congregational life.

We might ask ourselves what racial minorities would find attractive in UU congregations. Unitarian Universalism is historically a European, Caucasian faith tradition. We may wish it otherwise, but UU beliefs, customs, and traditions rarely hold interest for people of other races, national origins, and faiths. A member of my church who holds a Ph.D. once suggested that we acquire buses to bring black people from the inner city to our white suburban church, "Because they would learn so much from us." Aside from this astonishingly patronizing attitude, what exactly might racial minorities learn from UUs?

Also, why do we believe the direction should always be one-way, that others should come to us? Do black churches wonder why white people are not coming to worship? Do Chinese Baptists wonder why Hispanic Episcopalians are not joining?

The Task Force's insistence that new congregations be "anti-racist, anti-oppressive, and multi-cultural" (AR/AO/MC—new jargon) only bespeaks a wide chasm of ignorance about religion in America today. The Task Force planned for something that will never come to pass, under the model recommended here.

A Flawed Process from the Outset

Finally, I don't intend to single out the New Congregation Formation Task Force in my criticism of their recommendations. I suspect they followed the "charge" given to them, as have other denominational committees that drew faulty or wishful conclusions.

On the final page of the final Task Force report, a list of "stakeholders" (yet more jargon) who were interviewed for the study is presented. Seventeen UU groups are listed. It appears that the way we determine our future is for one group of UUs to ask another group of UUs what they think. We don't stop to question whether anyone is knowledgeable about the subject at hand.

We do not acknowledge that UUs are unaware of vast changes in the religious landscape that have taken place around us. As a movement, we are insular and isolated from the larger world of religion. We speak only among ourselves, and hopeful but unrealistic thinking is the result. Should we create fifty new large churches in five years? Sure, who wouldn't be in favor of that?

Unfortunately, the New Congregations report on starting fifty large churches exhibits a belief in the dream, "If we build it, they will come." This may be true in the movies, but not for Unitarian Universalism as it is configured today.

CHAPTER FOURTEEN

The UU Church
of the Future

HE UU CHURCH OF THE FUTURE will be unrecognizable from any UU church of today, and from any that has ever existed. Anyone now over fifty years of age may find the description of this church preposterous, but would probably enjoy going there, nevertheless.

Yet this church is an important key to our survival as a religious movement. It is the only church that will ever create the multicultural congregation that has forever eluded us. This church will draw on religious sources that UU's have not considered, and in fact have scorned. Yet these sources will be a wellspring of renewed religious faith. They will bring about a revival of Unitarian Universalism we have yearned for since our heyday in the nineteenth century.

About thirty years ago a UU minister told me he wanted to be the first minister on a space station. At the time I thought his wish was absurd. But today, people are living up there in space, with more on the way. Stranger things have happened.

Are you ready for a UU church of tomorrow? Here we go.

These churches will not have steeples, pews, organs, or stained glass windows. They are likely to be located in warehouses or other commercial sites. The people who come to these churches will be of all ages. These places will be noisy and boisterous, full of excitement and energy.

Worship will be highly participatory, like youth services at General Assembly today. People will stand close together, sing loudly, and perhaps have their arms about one another's shoulders. The music—jazz, blues, rock and roll—will be live, performed by first-rate professional musicians. The lighting will be colorful and dramatic.

Worship services will last for two or three hours, like services at Gospel churches today. After the service, people will stay and share a meal together, prepared by a high quality caterer. Potluck will be a relic of the past.

The highly involved worship style will draw from African American gospel churches and the Pentecostal movement. The theology of these churches will be multi-faceted as today, reflecting diverse beliefs. However, a significant part of the theology will be Pentecostal in nature—people sharing their personal experiences from the contemporary world in light of moral and ethical dilemmas they encounter.

These churches will not display only a "theology of entertainment." Young UU's have rejected the excesses of a consumer mentality, and their theology now includes a strict moral code of right and wrong, taken from religious and secular sources. This code includes abstinence from alcohol, drugs, and tobacco. Their religious values will be strong and unwavering.

Worship services will be conducted in two or three languages, alternating from one to another, with the text of hymns and prayers projected onto large screens so that all can take part. Rudimentary language classes will be offered before worship services so that all may participate to some extent. These churches will attract interracial couples, both straight and gay, bringing the mix that UU churches have not achieved to date.

Services will be held on Sunday mornings, in the afternoon, and in the evening. The church will also host mid-week services that start as late as 10:00 P.M. Smaller groups will also meet for worship in apartments and houses, reviving the "house church" model of worship.

These UU churches will draw from the success of "high demand" faiths of today, and will expect significant commitments of time and money from members. Tithing will be one of the expectations. The UU parents of these churchgoers will be shocked!

These churches will follow the advice of church-growth writer William Easum, and be "permission granting." They will not have a Board of Trustees to determine policy; the highly skilled paid staff will provide overall leadership. Young people in their twenties will be encouraged to create imaginative ministries on their own. The emphasis is on empowerment, not governance, just the opposite of UU churches today.

These young parishioners have money, energy, and technical expertise. Expect spectacular web sites, often entrepreneurial in nature, where people can purchase religious items, make charitable contributions, gain access to bulletin boards, discussion groups, BLOGS, and other instant communications.

These new UUs are part of the generation that is often described as civic-minded like their grandparents, except they are supremely confident that they have the resources and technical expertise to change the world in extraordinary ways.

These UUs will discard the notion of being church members and embrace a concept of discipleship. They do not seek self-understanding, but wish to be part of a completely different community with a completely different set of practices than UU churches today.

Among these new UUs, church "planters" will emerge. When a church reaches 800–900 members, half of them will break off and start a new church. Some congregations, however, may wish to become the first UU mega-churches with memberships of 2,500 or more, challenging the belief that theological diversity and large numbers of worshippers are incompatible goals.

These new congregations will send shock waves through the communities in which they minister because they will focus their efforts on a single cause—the least fortunate among us. Their model will be the Salvation Army, but without the requirement that recipients adopt a particular theology. These churches, like the new Ebenezer Baptist Church in Atlanta, will provide showers, clothing, and food to those who are in need; then expect them to attend worship with everyone else.

The people in these congregations will break the current cycle of those whose dominant image is being served, rather than to serve.

A well-trod path to Transylvania and other missions around the world will be a major characteristic of these churches. Young doctors and dentists will bring new levels of health care to rural villages. Engineers will help villages get running water. Architects and builders will help rebuild ancient churches. Scholarship funds will allow all Transylvanian youth to attend high school.

These new churches will draw newcomers because people will want to be associated with them. The ministers of these congregations realized long ago that the mission of the church could be stated simply: to change people's lives in some fundamental way. They will also realize that the vision of UU churches in the early years of the twenty-first century is not to promote the autonomy of the individual and to seek truth. Their vision is a deeper spirituality through service.

In addition to worship and service, this new model of church will offer educational programs taught by well-regarded academics, skilled practitioners, and people highly respected in their communities. These teachers, lecturers, and speakers will be generously compensated. Securing a teaching role in the church will be highly competitive. Only the best will do.

Younger generations have always been a revolutionary force among us. It may not have dawned on today's youth that they can revolutionize the church. But I hope they come to this realization soon— the sooner the better. Too much important work remains to be done, and this opportunity must not pass us by.

I hope people of all ages will be allies in this transition. Together, we can do far, far more than any of us have imagined.

REFERENCES

Introduction

1. George Barna, *The Second Coming of the Church* (Nashville: Word Publishing, 1998), 18.

Chapter One

1. Paul Wilkes, *Excellent Protestant Congregations* (Louisville: Westminster John Knox Press, 2001), 63.

Chapter Two

1. C. Peter Wagner, *Churchquake! How The New Apostolic Reformation is Shaking Up The Church As We Know It* (Ventura, CA: Gospel Light, 1998), 36.

2. Lyle Schaller, *Small Congregation, Big Potential* (Nashville: Abingdon Press, 2003), 20.

3. Miroslav Volf, "Way of Life," in *Christian Century* Magazine, Nov. 20–Dec. 3, 2002 issue, p. 35.

4. George Barna, *Evangelism That Works* (Ventura, CA: Regal Books, 1995), 51–52.

5. Rev. William Murry, from a sermon delivered at the UU Congregation at Shelter Rock, New York, on October 27, 2002.

6. John Shelby Spong, *Why Christianity Must Change or Die* (San Francisco: Harper Books, 1998), 66.

7. Anthony Robinson, *Transforming Congregational Culture* (Grand Rapids, MI: Eerdman's Publishing Company, 2003)

8. Robert Wuthnow, *The Crisis in the Churches: Spiritual Malaise, Fiscal Woe* (New York: Oxford University Press, 1999), especially chapters 7, 8, and 9.

9. Robinson, *Transforming Congregational Culture*, 89.

10. A. Powell Davies, *Without Apology: Collected Meditations on Liberal Religion*, edited by Forrest Church (Boston: Skinner House Books, 1998), 16.

Chapter Three

1. Robinson, *Transforming Congregational Culture*.

2. Robinson, 14.

3. Robinson, 18.

Chapter Four

1. Schaller, *Small Congregation, Big Potential,* 15.

Chapter Five

1. Philip Wiehe, *Ten Dumb Things Churches Do* (Harrisburg, PA: Morehouse Press, 2001), 17.

2. Dale Bullard, "When Things Get Tough, Blame the Denomination," *Net Results* Magazine, May/June 2003, 28–30.

3. Donald Miller, *Reinventing American Protestantism: Christianity in the New Millennium* (Berkeley: University of California Press, 1999), 11.

4. Miller, *Reinventing American Protestantism*, 17.

5. Miller, *Reinventing*, 12, 22.

6. Wagner, *Churchquake!*, 49.

7. Commission on Appraisal, *Reinventing Congregational Polity* (Boston: Unitarian Universalist Association, 1997)

8. Loren Mead, *More Than Numbers: The Ways Churches Grow* (Bethesda: The Alban Institute, 1993), 60–89.

9. James P. Wind, *The Leadership Situation Facing American Congregations* (Bethesda: The Alban Institute, 2001). An on-line version is available at no cost at Alban's website, **www.alban.org**

Chapter Six

1. Barna, *Second Coming of the Church*, 20.

2. Karl Barth quote from Thomas G. Long, "What Are They Asking?" *The Clergy Journal*, March 2003, 4–7.

Chapter Seven

1. Wagner, *Churchquake!*, 86.

Chapter Eight

1. Lyle Schaller, *The Very Large Church* (Nashville: Abingdon Press, 2000), 136.

2. Schaller, *The Very Large Church*, 226.

3. Rick Warren, *The Purpose Driven Church* (Grand Rapids: Zondervan Press, 1995)

4. Rick Warren, *The Purpose Driven Life* (Grand Rapids: Zondervan Press, 2003)

5. Wuthnow, *The Crisis in the Churches*, 239.

6. Commission on Appraisal, *Belongings* (Boston: Unitarian Universalist Association, 2000), 54.

7. Michael Foss, *Power Surge: Six Marks of Discipleship for a Changing Church* (Minneapolis: Augsburg Fortress Press, 2000), 73.

8. William Easum, *Sacred Cows Make Gourmet Burgers* (Nashville: Abingdon Press, 1995), 9.

9. Wilkes, *Excellent Protestant Congregations*, 159.

Chapter Ten

1. Ronald Heifitz, *Leadership Without Easy Answers* (Belknap Press, 1994)

2. Karen Fields, in the introduction to *The Elementary Forms of Religious Life*, by Emile Durkheim (New York: Free Press, 1995)

3. Lyle Schaller, *44 Ways to Expand the Financial Base of Your Congregation* (Nashville: Abingdon Press, 1989), 147.

Chapter Eleven

1. Wuthnow, *The Crisis in the Churches*, 56.

2. Arthur Simon, *How Much is Enough?* (Grand Rapids: Baker Books, 2003), 49.

3. John and Sylvia Ronsvalle, *The State of Church Giving,* Tenth Edition (Champaign, IL: empty tomb, inc. 2000)

4. Dean Hoge, Patrick McNamara, and Charles Zech, *Plain Talk About Churches and Money* (Bethesda: Alban Institute, 1997), 52.

Chapter Twelve

1. Arlin J. Rothauge, *Sizing Up a Congregation* (New York: Episcopal Church Center), 7–13.

Chapter Thirteen

1. New Congregations Task Force Report is available at **www.uua.org**.

2. Schaller, *The Very Large Church*, 97.